"Pastor Jonathan and I have a.. .... is the pastor of my home church. I was saved and discipled as a teenager at Wilcrest Baptist. It gives me great joy to see such a resource blossom from the place that changed my life. Jonathan does a great job of giving wisdom and application for families to be all that God desires. Too often we have subcontracted the church to disciple our families, thinking if we drop off our kids at church for a few hours they will have all the teaching needed to walk with Christ. The truth is church and home must act as a partnership. Parents are the primary disciplers and the church is the primary encourager. More can happen in the home seven days a week than at church one day a week. Allow Jonathan to teach you how to make your family a Gospel Family."

— **Gregg Matte, Pastor of Houston's First Baptist Church, Author of *Unstoppable Gospel***

"*Gospel Family* offers a clear path to move the gospel from the pages of the Bible and the church pews to the home. What a hopeful destination for our society that often calls the dysfunctional family functional and the broken home healthy. Jonathan Williams effectively weaves the ancient stories of the biblical families into the fabric of the present day home that desperately needs the healing power of the gospel. We are at a divine intersection that calls families to move toward clearly aligning with God's original design for the family. There are several practical steps for each family to take toward transforming the spiritual DNA of a family who desires to see worship, discipleship, and mission become as natural as eating a family meal, doing household chores, and experiencing a family movie night. Let me encourage you to take this exciting journey of faith to bring the gospel home."

— **Dr. Rodney Woo, Senior Pastor, International Baptist Church, Singapore, Author of *The Color of Church***

"The Introduction grabbed my heart and gave me hope that the hole in my own home and church might be filled with instruction and guidance to further take what I am doing as a lead pastor for a church, teaching the gospel and making disciples, into the homes of our body, as well as into my own home and family. I was not disappointed, and was greatly encouraged and challenged, by the clear content of this book. I'm excited to share this with our church community, and further apply these principles in my own family life as well."

— Jason Shepperd, Lead Pastor, Church Project,
The Woodlands, TX

"*Gospel Family* is much more than a book. It's a mission! Even among the 'biblically astute' there is sometimes a great disparity between God's Truth and personal experience. As a curriculum writer and speaker to men, it has always been my goal to help them not just fill in the blanks of a training guide, but to fill in the blanks of their life. This book will help you do exactly that with your *family*—fill in the blanks with the life-giving power of the gospel!"

— Tierce Green, Men's curriculum writer & speaker;
Co-presenter of *33 The Series*, a 6-volume Journey to
Authentic Manhood, Twitter: @tiercegreen

"*Gospel Family*, shares a journey that encourages families to cultivate Family Discipleship, Family Worship, and Family Missions in their home. This book models how discipleship becomes a partnership between family and church. Jonathan writes from his heart. His experiences as a missionary, pastor, husband, and father illustrate biblical principles which guide the book throughout. His words are both practical and inspirational. Many books of this type drift into theoretical language that seems unreachable by ordinary families. Gospel Family doesn't fall into this trap as it provides very useful words on worship, devotion, evangelism, and missions—all in the context of family. Discussion questions are helpful and provocative at times. I will recommend this one for families— particularly families with young children—as a way to lay a foundation of discipleship that will 'train up a child in the way they should go.'"

— **Dr. Alan Jackson, New Orleans Baptist Theological Seminary**

"My soul was deeply stirred as I read the pages of *Gospel Family*. The church is only as strong as the family. Our enemy hates the family and will do everything he can to destroy it. As a pastor, I have been waiting for a resource like this to help equip men and women in the church to live out their faith at home. Jonathan Williams has given us a robust and biblical defense of family God's way. *Gospel Family* is written to help a new generation of families catch the vision for a home where Christ is at the center."

— **Andrew Herbert, Lead Pastor, Taylor Memorial Baptist Church, Hobbs, New Mexico**

"Every Christian home would benefit from the insights in *Gospel Family* regardless of the type or size of your family. It is packed with relevant insights, suggestions, and resources that focus on developing the spiritual connections within your home. I was blessed by the real life illustrations and the emphasis on a Great Commission lifestyle. The wisdom contained in *Gospel Family* provides practical insights about the relationship between effective congregational worship and the intimacy of family worship at the kitchen table. Pastor Williams has shared his heart, his personal experience and his family journey in a way that allows Biblical wisdom to come to life."

— **Dr. Randy Jessen, Senior Pastor, Parker United Methodist Church, Parker, Colorado; Affiliate: Asbury Theological Seminary**

"Reading *Gospel Family*, I was inspired, encouraged, and challenged. Jonathan's book reminds us that our greatest ministry begins at home. Cultivating Gospel Families requires vision, time and sacrifice. This book reflects what I desire for my family as well as others."

— **Sidney Brock, Lead Pastor, Heritage Community Church, Fruitland Park, FL**

"Whether living in rich, first world countries or poor, third world slums, families and societies are in desperate need of the transforming power of the gospel. Hence, there is not a more timely and essential message both for the Church and the world than the need for Gospel Families. Jonathan Williams convinces us that the gospel is not simply bookends of our individual faith; it is the substance of our whole lives; and must serve as the foundation for any home. Prepare yourself to laugh, cry, and fall on your knees while reading this powerful and bold, yet extremely practical book. I pray a movement is birthed from the families affected by this work. I want my family to be a Gospel Family!"

— **William, Team Strategy Leader, South Asian Peoples, International Mission Board, SBC**

"*Gospel Family* is a much needed book today. It is easy to assume that believers know how to live for Christ at home, but the reality is that many families don't know how to do that and have never been trained. Jonathan gives his readers

iv

a strong theological foundation in *Gospel Family*, along with some practical ways to make Christ the center of the home. If you want to know what the Christian life can look like from Monday to Saturday, I encourage you to pick up this book."

— **Clint Kirby, Pastor of Gospel Church**
in Gdansk, Poland

"Strong families make strong churches and strong nations. Jonathan uses Biblical principles and relevant illustrations to help us lay a solid foundation and build strong Gospel Families. As a pastor, I want nothing more than each member of the church to be part of a loving, Christ centered family. *Gospel Family* will be one of the resources I use to teach families how to develop discipleship, worship and missions in the home."

— **Dan Rowland, Senior Pastor, Harrison Avenue**
Baptist Church, Harrison, Ohio

"Based firmly on Scripture, *Gospel Family* is full of practical, 'start it today' activities for husbands and wives seeking to build or strengthen Christ-centered marriages and for moms and dads working to intentionally disciple their children. Christian leaders will find *Gospel Family* useful for helping build Christ-centered families. Whether in one-on-one mentoring relationships or in small group Bible study, this resource is a great 'how-to' for families at any stage of their journey."

— **Mike Skaggs, Head of School,**
Trinity Christian Academy, Willow Park, TX

"*Gospel Family* touches two essential areas for society. Both a biblical Gospel and a clear structure for family life are

v

necessary in our current nuclear world. Jonathan's use of personal illustrations and life analogies bring the Gospel Family message alive. *Gospel Family* is a breath of fresh air for parents who want to establish a godly home as well as leave a legacy of Christ centered living for generations to come."

— Jim Grant, Senior Pastor Heartland Baptist Church, Alton, Illinois, DMin, Church Revitalization

"Jonathan Williams has a very challenging yet practical message for every family that desires to grow more rooted in the Word together as a family and enter into His presence through worship as a family. There is not a better resource for Christian families looking to instill gospel precepts into their homes than this book and gospelfamily.org. Both are a go to resource for me when I talk to parents who desire to take their families deeper in the Bible and in worship. This book perfectly explains the discipleship that God desires in our homes, neighborhoods, and across the world. I would recommend this book to anyone looking to invest eternal riches into their family!"

— Mason Pounds, NextGen Director, Valley Creek Church, Denton, TX

GOSPEL
FAMILY

CULTIVATING
FAMILY **DISCIPLESHIP,**
FAMILY **WORSHIP,**
& FAMILY **MISSIONS**

JONATHAN WILLIAMS

LUCIDBOOKS

Gospel Family

Copyrighted © 2015 by Jonathan Williams

Published by Lucid Books in Houston, TX.
www.LucidBooks.net

First Printing 2015

ISBN-13: 978-1-63296-021-4
ISBN-10: 1632960214

Special Sales: Most Lucid Books titles are available in special quantity discounts. Custom imprinting or excerpting can also be done to fit special needs. Contact Lucid Books at info@lucidbooks.net.

For Jess.

I am moved, inspired and blessed by your heart to see the Gospel in our home, and I praise the Lord for the way you passionately disciple our children and so many others. You are the love of my life and my favorite partner in the Gospel.

And for my parents who faithfully modeled a loving and gracious Gospel Family.

Table of Contents

Part One:
Casting a Gospel Family Vision for your Home

Part Two:
Cultivating Family Discipleship

The Gospel

THE GOSPEL IS THE BEAUTIFUL story of freedom and life through Jesus Christ, the Son of God.

It is a story that can become your story by grace through faith.

God, the Creator of everything, made people in His image. These same people, from the first man to us today, all people of every generation and every nation, have fallen short of God's holiness and have sinned against the One who created us.

Our sin leads to fear, guilt, shame, and death. Our sin separates us from the one, true, living God who made us in his image for his glory.

Fulfilling his promise to redeem this fallen, sinful world, God sent his only Son, Jesus Christ, to live a perfect, blameless, sinless life, and to seek and save the lost. Jesus took our fear, guilt, shame, sin, and death upon himself by dying on a wooden cross. He took our death that our sin deserved so that we may have his life; a new life; eternal life.

Three days after he was crucified on the cross, Jesus rose from the dead and lives forever, interceding for the church.

The Bible teaches that those, of any generation and of any nation, who repent of their sins and believe in Jesus Christ as their Lord, will be forgiven, freed and saved from fear, guilt, shame, and death.

Jesus promises that those who believe in Him will have eternal life with Him.

These are some passages from the Bible, God's Word to us, that celebrate this Gospel message:

- "Now I would remind you, brothers, of the Gospel I preached to you...that Christ died for our sins in accordance with the Scriptures, that he was buried, that he was raised on the third day in accordance with the Scriptures" (1 Cor. 15:1, 3-4).

- "For God so loved the world, that he gave his only Son, that whoever believes in him should not perish but have eternal life" (John 3:16).

- "For our sake he made him to be sin who knew no sin, so that in him we might become the righteousness of God" (2 Corinthians 5:21).

- "If you confess with your mouth that Jesus is Lord and believe in your heart that God raised him from the dead, you will be saved" (Romans 10:9).

- "For by grace you have been saved through faith. And this is not your own doing; it is the gift of God, not a result of works, so that no one may boast" (Eph. 2:8-9).

- "If we confess our sins, he is faithful and just to forgive us our sins and to cleanse us from all unrighteousness" (1 John 1:9).

- "If anyone is in Christ, he is a new creation. The old has passed away; behold, the new has come" (2 Corinthians 5:17).

Introduction

MY GRANDFATHER, CLYDE WILLIAMS, USED to own and operate Williams Furniture Store in Maryville, Tennessee, in the foothills of the Smoky Mountains. Although my grandfather has passed and the store has closed, I remember it well. I remember running behind the counter like I owned the place, playing with the measuring tape I found in the drawer by the cash register, and rocking with my brother in the wooden rocking chairs on display in the front window. We would pretend to be manikins as people passed by on the street.

My dad, David Williams, worked with Granddaddy Clyde as a young man and would even help with the deliveries. I guess it was then that my dad learned how to pack a truck and move any size furniture into any size house. Even still today, he helps my family whenever we move. I don't know how he does it, but he always finds the perfect way to pack the U-Haul, taking advantage of every space, fitting boxes in the truck like a master Tetris player. He's the guy putting boxes in the dryer and mirrors between the mattresses.

His days in the furniture store made him a moving genius. And it's not just the truck. You should see him when we get to the new house.

Couches that refuse to go through a doorway are masterfully angled and maneuvered in such a way that they effortlessly end up in the living room. Box spring mattresses that are unbendable, with no give, round corners like a snake slithering through the hallway. I look at these things and have no idea how to get them into the house, but with my dad's help, we find a way.

Most of us, even those of us who have been following Jesus for years, look at things like discipleship, worship, and missions, and have no idea how to get them into our homes. They seem to thrive in the church house. They seem to feel so natural and familiar when we're with our church. But when we talk about bringing them through the front door of our homes, they just don't seem to fit.

The prayer of Gospel Family Ministries is that we will come alongside families struggling to get the Gospel into their homes and become partners in this ministry. Just as my family could never move into a house without my dad's help and the help of many others, we could never be rooted in the Gospel without a community of believers. Gospel Family Ministries aims to provide the community, the resources, the prayer, and the encouragement needed to maneuver through the tight doorframes and narrow hallways in order to bring discipleship, worship, and missions into the home.

PART ONE

Casting a
Gospel Family Vision
for your Home

CHAPTER 1

Discovering the Biblical Foundation

Families Under Attack

I BELIEVE THAT THE ENEMY attacks the church, and I believe that he attacks the church by attacking the family. After all, the church is made up of families: families of all dynamics, from the grandparents raising their grandchildren and single moms to married couples adding children to their home every year and the single adult praying for a spouse. There are homes of one and homes of 21. The church consists of the adopting and adopted, the widowed and orphaned, the engaged and divorced, and many more. Family is diverse, and yet every home finds itself on common ground: attacked by the enemy.

As a pastor, I spend many of my days counseling these families: listening, praying, and walking through life together. Unfortunately, this gives me a front row seat to the attacks of the enemy who would destroy our homes and churches.

I've found myself standing with a wife outside her own house with a dozen police officers, as her husband barricaded himself inside; weeping with another in my office because her husband has filed for divorce; praying with one husband over his addiction to pornography and with another husband for his wife who spends her weekends going dancing with other men; watching one wife sign a new lease for an apartment because she doesn't trust her abusive spouse to be in the same home as her children, while praying over another family whose children's rebellious behavior has nearly destroyed the entire home.

One afternoon, the Lord burdened my heart for the family in a new way. I began to pray, seeking God's vision for the families of our church. Six months later, I preached a sermon entitled, "Gospel Families," and told our church that this would be the year of the Gospel Family. Three days later, I believe Christ spoke to me, calling me to invest in this ministry beyond just one vision for one church for one year. A month later, we launched Gospel Family Ministries.

Gospel Family Ministries is our response to the disparity between the Biblical portrait of family and the cultural portrait of family. We delight in the Scriptural vision of a family rooted in the Gospel of Jesus Christ and we mourn over the shattered families and broken homes that fill our communities. This disparity demands a response.

In the Beginning

I love stories, and I pay special attention to how stories begin. The first page of a book or the opening scene of a movie determines whether or not I'm hooked. Will I keep reading or watching?

James Barrie's *Peter Pan* grabs the reader with the first line, "All children, except one, grow up."[1] In the same way, the *Lion King* explodes onto the screen with a sunrise over the

African plains, accompanied by an African chant that none of us understand and yet we all recognize as the first verse of *The Circle of Life.*

The first two chapters of the Bible launch the greatest story ever told and immediately communicate two weighty truths for every home: (1) Family was designed with sacred intention, and (2) God is the divine designer. Our hopes to celebrate worship, missions & discipleship in the home are founded upon our belief that the Lord fashioned each person in our home in his image and for his purposes.

This is the beginning of the story; not just the creation of the heavens and the earth, not just the creation of man and woman, but the creation of the family. In the beginning, God created the family.

Jesus clearly recognized this spectacular truth about the origin of family.

When the Pharisees came to Jesus to test him about divorce, Jesus immediately brought it back to how it was in the beginning. He quoted Genesis 2:24 to emphasize the doctrine of one flesh and then said that their current practice of divorce was not in the original design (Matthew 19:3-8).[2]

Jesus turned the conversation back to the beginning of the story, giving his audience a renewal of the vows, so to speak, when they asked him about family, calling for a return to the original purpose of marriage.

We see the power of this whenever someone we know renews their wedding vows. Have you seen this? Have you seen the impact of a couple who has been married for decades, a couple who, between their wedding day and today has gone through storms of conflict and seasons of silence, stand up before their friends and family and say to one another, once again, their wedding vows? It's a return to the beginning; a reminder of their original intent, their first prayer for their family, the foundation they began with and have been building on ever since.

If we're going to lay a Biblical foundation for our families, we must follow Jesus' example of focusing on the beginning design of the family. Perhaps then we will catch God's vision for our homes.

God's Blueprint for Family

I believe that Genesis 1-2 is less about creation and more about the Creator. This is a passage not about the beauty of the heavens and the earth but about the beauty of God.

Throughout the creation narrative, God is revealed. As Psalm 19:1-2 says, "The heavens declare the glory of God, and the sky above proclaims his handiwork. Day to day pours out speech, and night to night reveals knowledge" (*see also Romans 1:19-20*).

Creation reveals God's eternal nature, for he exists before the beginning. It reveals his power as he creates everything out of nothing. It reveals his authority as he speaks light into being. It reveals his presence, as he is intimately involved in his creation, even naming the light, darkness, and sky. It reveals his goodness as he calls into existence, day after day, things that are divinely decreed as "*good.*" It reveals his provision as he provides oxygen, water, and food for every living creature he creates.

It reveals his creativity as he makes the fragrance of roses, the colors of the sunset, the crystals of the diamond, the force of an ocean wave, and the peaks of the Himalayas. It reveals his wisdom as he puts into place things like gravity, blood clotting, photosynthesis, human reproduction, thermodynamics, immune systems, solar systems, and DNA.

And it reveals his purpose as he fashions man and woman in his image for his sovereign reasons. How overwhelming to see God's purpose for his creation; to grasp his heart for marriage; for his blueprint for family to be exposed before us, that we might embrace it and bring it through the front doors of our homes!

God's design for the family is good (*Genesis 1:31*), and God's design for the family is one man, one woman, one flesh (*Genesis 1:22-24*). Let the family not just read the creation narrative as historians or theologians, but let us also engage this all-too-familiar story as architects delighting in the original plans of the Creator, that we may, by his grace, build a Gospel Family!

Paul sees the connection between the original design of the family and the Gospel of Jesus Christ. In Ephesians 5, Paul tells the church that Genesis 2:24—"A man shall leave his father and his mother and hold fast to his wife, and they shall become one flesh"—is referring to Christ and the church.

When a family comes together as one man, one woman, and one flesh, we see a picture of Christ and the church. We see the Gospel reenacted in the home.

Many families have reached this point. Many homes have the bones of the blueprint in place. There is one man, one woman, resembling, at least to some degree, one flesh. Maybe this is your home. But, perhaps, the bones of the blueprint have yet to be fleshed out. The Biblical foundation of the home doesn't stop with Genesis 2. The Bible reveals, even further, the depth of God's heart and God's design for the family.

Reshaping our View of Marriage

Some of the most famous stories are love stories: Romeo and Juliet, Cleopatra and Mark Anthony, Scarlett O'Hara and Rhett Butler, Pocahontas and John Smith, Titanic's Jack and Rose, Sam and Dianne of *Cheers*, Ross and Rachael of *Friends*, Jim and Pam of *The Office*, and the list goes on.

Genesis 24 tells the love story of Isaac and Rebekah.

After walking with God for more than 30 years, Abraham seems to be able to discern the Lord's will and pursues it, not just for himself, but also for his family. So he pursues this good thing for his son, this thing that he believes is fitting with God's will, and he pursues it with faith in the sovereignty and provision of the Lord.

Is your marriage a marriage that follows in faith? Are you more likely to be the spouse who encourages faithful following or the spouse who refuses to move when God calls?

After walking with God for more than 30 years, Abraham trusts in the provision and leading of the Lord, saying, "The Lord, the God of heaven...will send his angel before you, and you shall take a wife for my son from there."

Abraham does not take this marriage lightly.

He chooses his most faithful servant. He gives specific instructions. He seals it with an oath. He trusts it in the hands of the Lord. And the servant then travels about 520 miles, a 21-day journey, in order to find a wife for Isaac.

I married my bride, Jess, eight years ago, but it was eight years and seven months ago that I proposed. For those of you who don't know, a seven-month engagement means seven months of wedding planning. You have to choose a place for the ceremony and the reception, a dress for her, a tux for me, a song as she walks down the aisle, a song for our first dance, a song for our last dance, food for the reception, and, of course, cake.

Seven months to plan one night, and yet it's more than some spend planning for their life-long marriage. If we spend more time discussing the flowers than we do praying for the foundation of the marriage, then, perhaps, we are taking marriage lightly.

Our culture has cheapened marriage. What God designed as one man and one woman, what God designed as Gospel reenactment, we have taken and redefined, including everything from polygamy to same-sex marriages, and we have done away with the *one flesh* by viewing marriages as temporary.

If we hope to flesh out God's blueprint, reshaping our view of marriage, we are going to have to stop taking marriage lightly and begin praying for marriages faithfully.

In verse 12 of Genesis 24, Abraham's servant does pray for the marriage. He prays, "O Lord, God of my master Abraham, please grant me success today and show steadfast love to my master Abraham. By this I shall know that you have shown steadfast love to my master." He prays a specific prayer for Isaac's wife.

Prayer is the most important aspect of any relationship, whether it's one you have today or one you hope for tomorrow.

Have you ever watched people choosing vegetables at the grocery store? They don't rush. They don't run up and down the aisle carelessly throwing tomatoes, bananas, and grapefruit in their shopping cart. They take their time. Even the busiest people seem to just press "pause" on everything else going on in the world when they reach the produce aisle. They pick up the fruit or vegetable and examine it. They feel it, squeeze it, and even smell it before deciding whether or not they want it. It makes me wonder: do we put more thought and examination into choosing tomatoes than we do in selecting a spouse? Are we praying for God's will for the person we will marry? For the person our children will marry? Are you currently praying God's will for your spouse?

When Rebekah enters the story, we immediately see that this will not be an ordinary marriage, for she is no ordinary woman. Rebekah demonstrated purity and a servant heart, even drawing enough water to care for 10 camels. I've heard, by the way, that camels are able to store up to 30 gallons of water each. Now, we don't know if these camels were running on *empty* or if they still had a quarter of a tank, but regardless, drawing enough water for 10 camels must have taken some time.

A servant heart is at the root of a Gospel Family marriage, for Ephesians 5:25, reads, "Husbands, love your wives, as Christ loved the church and gave himself up for her."

While selfishness pollutes marriages, selflessness blesses marriages.

Rebekah and her servant heart were answers to prayer and so the servant worshiped God for this answered prayer and for his steadfast love and faithfulness (he even gave Rebekah bracelets and a nose ring, which is a bit different than the wedding ring I gave my wife). Even Rebekah's family recognized the Lord's sovereign hand in this marriage, acknowledging that this was a divinely arranged marriage, reminding us that marriage is not something we create or orchestrate, but it is the Lord's gracious gift. As Proverbs 18:22 teaches: "He who finds a wife finds a good thing and obtains favor from the Lord."

Our view of marriage is weak. Our expectation of marriage is weak. As the church, we claim to be the ones in this nation elevating a Biblical view of marriage and yet far too many of the marriages within the church settle for the cultural standard for marriage. Should we not desire more, expect more? Should we not plead in prayer for a marriage divinely arranged and sovereignly orchestrated by God? Should we not wait for loving, serving spouses who are an answer to years of prayers? Should we not expect the Lord to refine us all to be Gospel Families?

A Family that Grows Daily

I have a spot in my closet with pencil markings. Most of you have this spot somewhere in your house too. It's the place where I take my kids once a year to measure their height. They stand against the wall and I draw a line at the top of their heads. I write their names and the date by their line so that we can compare it with last year's mark. My kids love seeing the change from year to year.

My wife and I think they may be growing up too fast, but we praise God that they are indeed healthy and growing year after year. This is our prayer after all. In fact, so much of what we do is invested in their physical growth and health.

We feed them throughout the day, teach them to brush their teeth, make sure they take naps, and constantly give them baths, vitamins, Band-Aids, medicine, and—in my son's case—haircuts. Sy's hair grows so fast and thick that we have to cut it just so his hats will still fit.

Most families invest in the *physical* growth and health of their children, and yet most families neglect the *spiritual* growth and health of their children. We limit it to Sundays, as though nourishment given once a week is sufficient. Would we ever limit our family's meals or vitamins or baths or medicine to once a week?

John Stott describes this spiritual growth as a responsibility, while observing, "The tragedy is that many Christians, genuinely born again in Christ, never grow up. Others even suffer from spiritual infantile regression. Our heavenly Father's purpose, on the other hand, is that 'babies in Christ' should become 'mature in Christ.' Our birth must be followed by growth."[3]

A Gospel Family founded upon God's Word will be a family that grows together spiritually every single day.

After giving his people the greatest commandment in Deuteronomy 6:4-5, God says, "These words that I command you today shall be on your heart. You shall teach them diligently to your children, and shall talk of them when you sit in your house, and when you walk by the way, and when you lie down, and when you rise. You shall bind them as a sign on your hand, and they shall be as frontlets between your eyes. You shall write them on the doorposts of your house and your gates" (Deuteronomy 6:6-9).

This is a family saturated with the Word of God. This is a family who invests in the spiritual growth and health of their home in the morning, afternoon, and evening. This is a family that grows daily.

Their hearts bear the Word of God. Their children delight in the Word of God. Their homes are decorated with the Word of God.

Stott challenges the Christian family to allow the Word of God to mature us when he writes, "Our relationship to our heavenly Father, though secure, is not static. He wants his children to grow up to know him more and more intimately. Generations of Christians have discovered that the best way to do this is to spend time with him every day in Bible reading and prayer."[4]

Right after college, I served two years as a missionary in the Amazon Jungle. We traveled up and down a Peruvian river in a small canoe, taking the Gospel to a previously unreached indigenous people group, the Amarakaeri. The Amarakaeri are a small tribe of families that live primarily in six different villages in the jungle. Since they were not familiar with the Word of God, we began sharing the Gospel by storying chronologically through the Old and New Testaments.

The nights were the best time for the entire village to get together. The men would return from hunting, fishing, or farming, the kids would come in from their soccer game or their afternoon swim, and the women would take a break from their daily chores. Then, underneath the hut, often by the fire, we would walk through the Gospel, story by story, and celebrate the glory of Christ.

Some of the most beautiful pictures of the church I've encountered came during these nights, and whenever I meditate on Gospel Families, I'm reminded of that tribe, those "hut churches," sitting there together, husbands, wives, teenagers, children, babies, even a few random animals (one lady never went anywhere without her pet monkey camped out on top of her head, using her hair as his blanket) worshiping as a family, talking about their day and the Scriptures interchangeably, for Christ touched every aspect of life.

These families were not perfect, and neither was the church. But as they matured in their faith month after month, the Word of God dug deeper and deeper into the foundation of their hearts, with roots that stretched from one corner of the home to the other, from sunrise to sunset.

Our homes are to be homes founded upon the Word of God. Our families are to be families that grow daily. Our mornings, afternoons, and evenings are to be spent teaching the Gospel, living the Gospel, modeling the Gospel, proclaiming the Gospel.

How do we do this?

4 Steps to Rooting your Family in the Gospel

Cast a Vision: In the next chapter, your family will have a chance to formulate a mission statement and cast a Gospel Family vision for your home. This includes the broken homes seeking a vision for restoration. After recognizing God's Biblical design for family, this is the first step to establishing this Biblical foundation for your home. Gospel Families don't happen on accident or by chance. I've never seen anyone just stumble into this sort of reality. There must be intentionality. There must be prayer. And there must be a godly vision.

Celebrate Discipleship: When the Great Commandment is obeyed, we see one believer loving the Lord with all of his or her affections. When the Great Commandment is reproduced, we find that one believer leading others, beginning with family, to also love the Lord with all their heart, soul, strength, and mind. Family Discipleship occurs when this love for Christ is modeled and reproduced in the home.

Delight in Worship: The purpose of every home is to bring glory to God. This should move us to be families that worship together. Anyone who aims to root their family in the Gospel will invest their days worshiping God, delighting in his presence.

Partner in Missions: The Great Commission is not just for missionaries and it's not just for churches. It's for families. It's a call to make disciples, to begin with the people in your home, and then to see your family as partners in the gospel, partners in the Great Commission. When this becomes a joy, not a burden, when this becomes natural, not manufactured, and when this becomes intentional, not left to chance, we can truly say that missions is part of the foundation of the home. With this foundation, your family can be a force God uses to redeem the world he created.

Throughout the rest of the book, we will unpack these four steps in hopes of seeing a revival in the home, so that no matter what your starting point is today, your next season will find your family further embracing and living a Gospel Family vision.

Family Discussion Questions

1. Did you grow up in a home of one man, one woman, and one flesh?

2. What did you see in your home growing up that you want to avoid in your home?

3. What did you see that you want to reproduce in your home today?

4. What are some of the worldly things that have corrupted the good family God created?

5. What would need to change in your family for your home to reflect the Gospel?

CHAPTER 2

Developing a Mission Statement

Family Identity

SOME OF MY FAVORITE MOVIES are the Bourne movies, starring Matt Damon as Jason Bourne, based on the Robert Ludlum novels: The Bourne Identity, The Bourne Supremacy, and The Bourne Ultimatum.

In the first movie, The Bourne Identity, CIA assassin Jason Bourne wakes up in a boat with amnesia. He spends most of the movie wondering who he is. He has a stack of passports, all with different names, and sets out to find someone who knows his real identity, someone who can tell him who he really is.

Until we meet Christ, we all have identity amnesia, and there are stacks of passports out there, crowds of people, ready to tell us our name, ready to tell us who we are. Then one day, we find the one who was there in the beginning, the one who wove us together in our mother's womb. He tells us who we are in him and he gives us a new name.

Every family has an identity as well, and every family has a name. In fact, those around us will tell us we get to choose

17

this name. There is a stack of options for your home that the world freely offers. You can be the rich family with the largest house on the block. You can be the busy family whose car is only in the driveway long enough to reload before the next activity. You can be the sports family known for tailgating and March Madness. You can be the isolated family that sticks to itself. You can be the gossip family, the depressed family, the nosey family, the funny family, the garage sale family, or the game night family.

We can either take our home to the world and let it define our vision, our identity, and give us a nametag for our family to wear, or we can bring our homes to Christ and allow him to define us, give us our identity, and create a new vision within our home.

Nehemiah Days

In the first pages of the Old Testament book of Nehemiah, the cupbearer to the king receives some news. This was long before newspapers, Facebook status updates, and Twitter. The news came firsthand and in person, as one of his brothers came to Susa the citadel and met with Nehemiah. Nehemiah asked him about the remnant of Jews still left in Jerusalem and about the city itself.

The report was crippling.

One of my friends, Paul Simon, a Haitian American, shared a similar experience back in January, 2010. On the 12th of that month, a catastrophic, 7.0 earthquake shattered Paul's home nation of Haiti. Paul lived in Houston at the time and, with many of his family members still living in Haiti, this news was absolutely devastating.

It's heartbreaking to hear that your home has been shaken. Nehemiah felt this heartbreak. Scripture says that he immediately "sat down and wept and mourned for days, and continued fasting and praying before the God of heaven."

If you're familiar with the story, you'll remember that Nehemiah, the cupbearer to the king, goes to the king and asks permission to return to Jerusalem, the broken city, with gates destroyed by fire.

Nehemiah writes, "The king granted me what I asked, for the good hand of my God was upon me."

So Nehemiah returns to Jerusalem, but says nothing to the people there about his vision for the city. He stays there for three days without saying a word. There's no meeting, no prayer gathering, and no mission statement. Instead, he spends those three days inspecting the brokenness. It's a time of examination. He needs to see with his own eyes the burnt gate, the broken walls, even traveling to the point that he can no longer keep moving for the piles of rubble.

Then he speaks. And he speaks boldly. He stands up, in front of the Jews, the priests, the nobles, and the officials, and he casts a vision, a courageous, valiant vision. Fearlessly, Nehemiah says, "Come, let us build the wall of Jerusalem."

He couldn't have been clearer. He couldn't have been more daring.

Our families need this sort of dauntless determination; this sort of bold vision casting.

Like Nehemiah, it is time for our families to invest in prayer, fasting, and examination; to inspect the corners of our homes, the broken places, burnt spots, and areas of rubble. Let us spend three days seeking God's heart for our home and then let us stand up with passion and resolve and clearly lay before our family a Gospel Family mission that we aim to pursue.

The first step, then, to developing a Gospel-centered mission statement for our home, one that will lead us to find our new identity in Christ, is to have some Nehemiah days of prayer, fasting, examination, and vision casting.

The pastor of Houston's First Baptist Church, Gregg Matte, also encourages a time of examination before casting vision. He writes, "In leading a group toward God's will, you must first know where you are. Take a clear look at your family...a strong, truthful assessment of the present is crucial to leading them into the future." Matte reminds us, "Vision is understanding the past and the present in order to lead a group into the future."[5]

Preparing for the Mission

One of my closest friends serves with his family as missionaries in India. They work primarily with Islamic communities, sharing Christ with the Muslims of their city. It's a hot, crowded, intense place filled with a host of idols and false religions. And not too long ago, I had the chance to go there for one week to serve alongside this faithful team of missionaries to see what the Lord is doing on the other side of the world.

I had never been to India or served so intentionally with Islamic families, and it was certain to be my longest flight yet.

I began preparing months before takeoff. I received three new shots and a Malaria prescription, read a few books on the Islamic faith, Skyped with the missionaries there often with an onslaught of questions, invested much time in prayer, ate some new Indian dishes with a few of my Indian friends here in the States, and loaded up on books for the long flight.

When we are called to a mission, whether a trip to India, a new job, or pursuing revival in the home, we are called to prepare. So let me put forth some questions to help you prepare for a Nehemiah-like vision of pursuing a Gospel Family. Take some time over the next three days and actually write down your answers in hopes of examining your greatest needs, most urgent prayer requests, and the path your family needs to take.

What do you believe the Lord desires for your home this year?

What is your vision for your family's spiritual growth and discipleship?

What is your role in this vision?

What are five core values your family prizes?

Read Galatians 5:19-21: "Now the works of the flesh are evident: sexual immorality, impurity, sensuality, idolatry, sorcery, enmity, strife, jealousy, fits of anger, rivalries, dissensions, divisions, envy, drunkenness, orgies, and things like these." *Which of these exist in your home and need to be removed by the power of the Spirit of Christ?*

Read Galatians 5:22-23: "The fruit of the Spirit is love, joy, peace, patience, kindness, goodness, faithfulness, gentleness, self-control." *What godly characteristics would you like to see strengthened in your family members?*

What are three goals you can set in order to see worship (devotions, prayer, singing praises, Bible study, serving together…) become more evident in your family & home?

What challenges do you expect to encounter as you try to implement these goals and vision?

What will help you reach these goals and fulfill this vision?

I believe that three days of praying through this reflection, as you seek God's heart in Scripture, will find you arriving at the family identity the Lord has for you as well as the path you need to take to get there. I encourage you to produce a family mission statement that you can display in your home and pursue together. Write it down, post it on the refrigerator, paint it on the wall, frame it in the living room. Inject it into family conversations and teachable moments. Make it a central part of your family's story. Share it with friends and use it to describe your family when you meet someone new.

Welcome the Uncomfortable

When we encounter a God-sized vision, it can be uncomfortable. Hearing his voice and discerning his will, can leave us feeling stretched and challenged and moved in unfamiliar ways.

I'm reminded of Jacob who wrestled with God and how this one encounter did not leave him unchanged, but limping for the rest of his life. With every painful, uncomfortable step, he was reminded of that encounter. And yet I imagine it was a welcomed discomfort, for it was a feeling of reassurance of God's presence.

You see, not all discomfort is bad and not all comfort is good. Often, we are comfortable with sinful things, worldly things, and we need an encounter with God that does not leave us unchanged. We need to walk away limping, with a gracious discomfort.

The one who can sit on the couch all day and just watch TV and eat junk food might say he's comfortable, but it's clear that something needs to change because he shouldn't be so comfortable with such laziness.

The one who can treat his wife like a stranger might be comfortable ignoring her, but it's clear that it's time for this man to move outside his comfort zone and love his bride like Christ loves the church.

The one who is quite comfortable with her own gossip needs the Lord to touch her heart until gracious speech becomes her new normal.

Those who feel comfortable with their addiction to pornography, drugs, or alcohol, would be blessed by the touch of Christ that brings them to a place of discomfort every time they're around these things, so that their satisfaction would only be found in Christ.

As we ask Jesus to touch our families, let us welcome the uncomfortable, allowing his Spirit to stretch and change our homes and to reveal the areas of sinful comfort that need to be broken.

Active Waiting

Even the healthiest of families will find areas in their homes where spiritual growth is needed. Families will recognize spots where discipleship, worship, or missions could be strengthened, more consistent, or more joyful. All of us could hear a new mission from the Lord for our homes, and the truth is, this can be overwhelming.

Seeing the difference between where we are and where we want to be can leave us discouraged, like when we have to keep zooming out on our phone's GPS just to see the entire route between our green dot (where we are) and the red dot (where we're going). That long blue line taunts us as it stretches across our entire screen, as though our cell phone battery will die before we complete our charted journey.

I pray against this discouragement. I pray against a sense of the impossible. I pray against a feeling of failure before you even begin. I pray against fear that your family won't follow, doubt that anything can change, and guilt that you haven't done all of this already.

This book is not meant to make you feel guilty for waiting until now to further root your home in the Gospel. This book is meant to celebrate the beauty of a Gospel-rooted home so that all of us will fall in love with the vision of pursuing these things together as a family.

And the mission statement is not one that is impossible but, rather, one of faith and dependence. We have faith that

Christ can move us from that green dot to the red dot and we openly recognize our daily dependence on him to be both the GPS that guides us and the engine that moves us.

I am privileged to pastor Wilcrest Baptist Church, a multi-ethnic church in Houston, Texas. We have more than 50 nations gather each week to worship. However, it hasn't always been like this. Back in 1992, Wilcrest was a predominately white church settled in an increasingly diverse neighborhood. The church was without a pastor and praying about calling a 29-year-old man, Dr. Rodney Woo, to shepherd them through the next season.

Pastor Rodney took his Nehemiah moment and, after prayer and examination, cast a vision for a multi-ethnic church. The homogenous church embraced the vision, called Pastor Rodney, and began a seemingly impossible journey. Dr. Woo tells this 18-year-long story in his inspiring book, *The Color of Church*.[6]

During his first year at Wilcrest, Pastor Rodney took about 40 of the members of the church on a prayer retreat. The main goal of their weekend was to formulate a mission statement. They returned to the church with a new vision that has served as the heartbeat for more than 20 years: "*Wilcrest Baptist Church is God's multi-ethnic bridge that draws all people to Jesus Christ who transforms them from unbelievers to missionaries.*"

In those early years, the church would stand each Sunday and say the mission statement together. It was an exercise in unity, faith and dependence. And it was a little bit funny. It was funny because the all-white church would stand and say that they are "God's multi-ethnic bridge," and as they looked around, there wasn't anything "multi-ethnic" about them. But they didn't let the distance between their reality and their vision discourage them. The blue line between the two dots seemed longer than ever, but their faith in God was stronger than ever.

This is active waiting. It's waiting because we're not there yet and we are anticipating the Lord's unseen movement. It's active because we're not just sitting around doing nothing but, rather, we are obeying God's call for today, praying and depending upon him, trusting that he will use a string of these days to bring about his will in his timing.

It may seem a little funny to say your mission statement together as a family when your reality falls far short of the vision. This is simply a reminder of our season of active waiting; of coupling faith with dependence.

We find ourselves in a long line of faithful followers when we aim for this sort of transformational mission. It's a legacy of believers who understood that the impossible is not impossible for the one who can heal the blind and calm the storm. These faithful all embraced the Lord's vision for their lives, chasing a new mission statement, a new name.

It's Matthew going from being the Great Collector to the one who would record the Great Commission.

It's Peter no longer needing his boat because he's now with the one who can walk on water.

It's John dropping his nets, trusting his needs to the one who can feed the 5,000.

It's the empty woman at the well being filled with living water.

It's Lazarus discovering that death doesn't have the last word.

It's the thief finding healing even as he bleeds to death on the cross.

It's Saul going blind in order to see for the first time. And it's your family opening up the front door of your home to a Gospel-centered vision. This is the sort of transformation we've needed, the revival for which our souls have longed.

So instead of taking the current state of your home to the world, to the stack of passports and identities available, asking for your name, your identity, your mission, let us, in faith and dependence, go to Christ prayerfully, receive our mission and start the journey.

Family Discussion Questions

1. What type of family do you have?
2. What would your family pray for if you had a day of fasting and examination?
3. What mission do you believe Jesus has for you and your family?
4. Have you ever followed the Lord into something that stretched you beyond your comfort zone? How would you describe this experience?

CHAPTER 3

Shepherds in the Home

Shepherds Follow the Shepherd

SOMEONE IS LEADING YOUR FAMILY. Right now, as you read, your home has a leader. Even if you're the only one in your home, there is a leader, and it might not be you. If there are many people in your home, you may find that there are many leaders as well.

If we accept this premise—that every home, every family, is following someone—are we willing to leave the identity of that leader to chance? Do we care who has the heart and attention of our family? Are we concerned with how they're leading or where they're taking them?

How do we ensure that our family has the right leader?

First, we must proclaim that the Shepherd we need to lead our families is Jesus Christ, the Good Shepherd. He's the one who made us, knows us, loves us, provides for us, protects us, and lays down his life for us, his sheep. He's the only one who can lead, for he's not just the one who knows the way we need to go, but, in his words, he *is* the way (John 14:6). And if he is to be the Shepherd of our homes, then we need family shepherds who will follow the Good Shepherd and lead the rest of the family to do the same.

Simply put, every family needs a shepherd who follows Christ and leads the rest of the family to follow him too.

As John Piper writes, "All true spiritual leadership has its roots in desperation."[7]

In his book on *The Shepherd Leader at Home*, author Timothy Witmer calls the spiritual leader of the home to, first of all, follow Christ. He writes, "In leading our families we must be motivated by love for the Lord and for the well-being of our loved ones. It must be evident to them that it matters to us that we are following the Good Shepherd ourselves and putting godly principles into practice in our own lives."[8]

What we need is a Joshua.

Shepherds Highlight God's Presence

In the final chapter of the book of Joshua, Moses' successor stands up and addresses the people. Joshua begins by recounting the faithfulness of God, chronologically tracing the history of the people and their encounters with God. He highlights God's presence with his people, tracing the miraculous and delivering work of God from the call of Abram, through the Exodus from Egypt and the wandering in the wilderness, all the way to the conquest of the Promised Land.

Then comes verse 14: "Now, therefore, fear the Lord and serve him in sincerity and truth" (Joshua 24:14).

Verse 14 is a natural response to God's history with his people. It's like saying, since God is always faithful, always good, always sovereign, since he always keeps his word, since he always protects and provides, it seems fitting that we should serve this faithful God faithfully.

I gave testimony earlier to the diversity of our church. It's a joy to see so many nations singing praises to Christ together.

Sometimes, groups from other churches or seminaries come to visit and worship with us so that they can see this picture of the nations glorifying the Lord as one body. I'm honored to be a part of this small witness of Revelation 7:9, but I would never want these visitors to leave our church excited about our diversity. I want them to leave excited about Jesus. As I share with our church, we don't want our church to highlight diversity, we want our diversity to highlight Christ and his gospel. We want to tell others of God's faithful history and demonstrate an appropriate response.

This should be the aim of every household. Just as Joshua pointed the people to a long history of God's goodness and unswerving, steadfast presence and provision, our families are to highlight Christ and the gospel, giving unbroken testimonies of his presence in our lives.

Joshua's call was in response to what God had already done. What has God done in your life? What has the Lord accomplished for your family? How has he provided for your home? From what disasters has he delivered you? When was a time that he made himself known?

Let us meditate on the Lord's presence in our lives, and let us respond appropriately, namely, by fearing and serving the Lord.

Every Thanksgiving, my family sits at the table, eyeballing the turkey and dressing while making a mental note of how long we have until the Dallas Cowboys kickoff, and then it happens. We do it every year. I don't know who started this tradition, though I suspect many families do the same thing every Thanksgiving. We take turns going around the table mentioning one thing we're thankful for from the past year.

Gracie, my little girl, might say a prayer of thanksgiving for our new baby, Elijah, as well as her trampoline and tiaras, while our younger son, Silas, will thank the Lord for his mommy, Batmobile, and donuts.

Throughout Scripture, God's people are called to remember.

David embraced this call to remember the good works of God. He writes, "My soul will be satisfied as with fat and rich food, and my mouth will praise you with joyful lips, when I remember you upon my bed, and meditate on you in the watches of the night; for you have been my help, and in the shadow of your wings I will sing for you" (Psalm 63:5-7).

Our family time of remembering should not come only once a year. We shouldn't wait until next Thanksgiving to lead our children, the next generation, in a time of remembering, a time of praising Christ for his good works in our life. We are to meditate and reflect upon his provision, faithfulness, healing, goodness, comfort, guidance, and answered prayers daily, "in the watches of the night," so that our families will set their hope in God and not forget His miracles.

How do we do this? Well, tonight, when you sit down to eat dinner or as you're putting your children into their beds, give each family member a chance to remember the goodness of God and then lead your family in a prayer of praise, for we need Joshuas who will highlight the presence of the Lord in our homes.

Shepherds Lead their Families to Get Rid of Idols

Every family has a leader, someone or something they follow, and any leader not following Christ is nothing short of an idol. Tragically, this means that most homes are filled with idols, for few families sincerely claim to be following the Good Shepherd, submitting their schedules, money, children, and goals to the will of Jesus.

Have you ever walked into a home of a family that blatantly and proudly displays their idols? I have. I've seen altars to false gods, shelves lined with man-made objects of worship, and prayer pillows in front of shrines—worn-out prayer pillows at that.

It's staggering to see such an unashamed, prominent,

public display of idols. It's staggering, not because idolatry in the home is uncommon, but because most of us hide our idolatry, like Rachel sitting on her father's stolen gods in the tent (Gen. 31:34).

After calling the people to respond to the Lord's long history of faithfulness, Joshua makes another exhortation: "And put away the gods which your fathers served beyond the River and in Egypt, and serve the Lord. If it is disagreeable in your sight to serve the Lord, choose for yourselves today whom you will serve: whether the gods which your fathers served which were beyond the River, or the gods of the Amorites in whose land you are living."

Joshua leaves the people with two options: Either serve God or serve false gods. Either worship the God who has revealed himself as personal, powerful and faithful, or serve dead idols made by man. Joshua is clear that to choose idols over God is to say, with your actions, that worshiping the true God is evil in your sight. We aren't usually this clear and bold in our definition of idolatry. We usually water it down, but make no mistake about it, idolatry, putting anything in the place of God, worshiping anything or anyone instead of God, reveals our sinful heart and the fact that we actually consider true worship of the true God as disagreeable and evil.

This is an appropriate and necessary admonition for Joshua to make, for at the beginning of this chapter, as he is storying through their relationship with the Lord, they are reminded that Abram's father Terah served other gods, the false gods of Mesopotamia. Furthermore, the location of this covenant renewal is Shechem, which was previously a center of pagan worship.

While we aren't descendants of Terah and don't live in Shechem, the call to shepherd our families to get rid of idols remains an appropriate admonition for us today. Most of us can identify temptations for idolatry in our homes. One way to identify these temptations is to examine how we devote our time. For example, what receives the greatest attention and conversation in your home? TV? Sports? School? Social Media? Video Games? Yard work? Eating? Vacation? Retirement?

There is another story in the Bible that parallels Joshua's challenge to get rid of idols, and, while it took place hundreds of years earlier, it was in the same city of Shechem. In Genesis 35, Jacob prepares his family to go and dwell with God in Bethel, but before they can leave they have some unpacking to do.

When my family goes on a trip, we don't unpack. We pack. Even my children get into the packing. My daughter fills her backpack with stuffed animals, books, and dress-up clothes, trusting that she is now prepared for anything. My son, Silas, takes a different approach, focusing on his Ninja Turtles and Super Heroes, before grabbing bags of Gold Fish crackers and Cheetos from the pantry. He'll pretty much pack all the food from the lowest shelf, all he can reach.

Jacob doesn't pack for his trip, though. He unpacks. He tells his family to, "put away the foreign gods that are among you." We know his wife Rachel had stolen her father's gods and that his sons had just plundered an entire city, likely taking their idols as well. Jacob had allowed these idols in his home for about ten years, but if they are to dwell with God, it's time to get them out of the house and bury them under the terebinth tree.

In the late 16th century, a Japanese warlord had 50,000 men spend five years building a colossal statue of Buddha for a shrine in Kyoto. Soon after it was finished, an earthquake hit the city, the roof of the shrine came crashing down and the idol was destroyed.[9]

I don't know how long you've been worshiping your idols or how long it's taken for them to become rooted in your life and home, but I do know that it is time they all come crashing down. It's time to bury them under the tree in the backyard.

Will you lead your family, shepherd your home, to clean out the idols of your home?

Shepherds Lead their Families to Worship the Lord

Before the people can even decide whether or not they will get rid of their idols to serve the faithful God, Joshua sets the example and says the famous words, "As for me and my house, we will serve the Lord" (Joshua 24:15).

The word here for "serve" not only means to *serve* but also to *worship*. As a shepherd leader in his home, Joshua speaks first and is the first one to commit his family to be a family that highlights God's presence, expels any idols, and worships the Lord. He commits himself and his family to a life of worshiping the one, true, living God.

Fathers, husbands, have you done this for your family yet? Have you prayerfully and boldly made the commitment to lead your family to worship God? Are you leading your family to revere God, put away idols, and serve Jesus Christ? This doesn't mean you're perfect, but it does mean you're intentional.

Gospel Families will never emerge accidentally. Gospel Families don't happen by chance, and neither does spiritual leadership. It takes boldness. It requires commitment. It calls for intentionality. Some families spend more time talking about what to eat for dinner than they do talking about how to serve God together as a family. Some families are very intentional in how they will save for college or spend their retirement or where they'll go on vacation, but they leave the most important thing to chance.

The spiritual well being of your family should not be left to chance.

We need spiritual leadership.

We need family shepherds.

We need Joshuas, who will stand up and intentionally choose to lead their homes to worship Christ.

Spiritual leaders lead their homes and others to saving faith in Jesus. When Paul instructs Titus to appoint elders in the church, he lists qualifications of the church overseer, including the leader's family life and home. Paul specifies that the children of the church elders are to be "believers and not open to the charge of debauchery or insubordination" (Titus 1:6). Paul recognizes that those who lead outside the home must first lead inside the home. Those who would disciple others must first disciple their family members. As Paul writes to Timothy, "He must manage his own household well, with all dignity keeping his children submissive, for if someone does not know how to manage his own household, how will he care for God's church?" (1 Timothy 3:4-5).

Pastor Voddie Baucham reflects on Paul's instructions to Titus and Timothy, concluding, "It's impossible to overstate the importance of the ministry of the home in the pastoral Epistles. Again and again we find admonitions to parents and children and instructions to elders that center on the disciple-making function of the family, and particularly the family shepherd."[10]

A Word for Husbands and Fathers

The Bible clearly teaches that God made both man and woman in his image and that both have divine roles and callings in the family and home. I will explore the beauty of this partnership more in chapter 12, for I do see the entire family as partners in the Gospel, living the mission together. I also believe that as the Scriptures present some of the varying responsibilities of husbands and wives, husbands are called to the joyful responsibility of spiritually leading their families.

I see this Biblically in passages like Ephesians 5:23-24, which reads, "For the husband is the head of the wife even as Christ is the head of the church, his body, and is himself its Savior. Now as the church submits to Christ, so also wives should submit in everything to their husbands" (see also Colossians 3, 1 Peter 3, Titus 2, Genesis 1-3 and 1 Corinthians 11).

In the same way, Ephesians 6:4 calls fathers to be the Joshuas, the shepherd leaders of the home, charging, "Fathers, do not provoke your children to anger, but bring them up in the discipline and instruction of the Lord."

As the husband of a beautiful, gifted, passionate woman of God and follower of Christ, and as the father of three wonderful children, I know that this call to lead can be overwhelming. After all, as a husband, I am commanded to love my bride as Christ loves his bride, the church, and I am reminded that Christ loved his bride by dying for her, sacrificing everything, covering her with an unconditional love.

Pastor Eric Mason puts this in perspective, writing, "The husband's role is to reflect Jesus' self-denying death as he helps the spiritual growth of his wife."[11]

As a father, I am ever aware that my example is God, our Heavenly Father. Even the best fathers are mere glimpses of the perfect Father, while the worst fathers are mere reminders of our desperate need for the Heavenly Father.

While I was in seminary, one of my professors wrote an essay that addressed the call of the father in the realm of making disciples in the home. He wrote, "The father's responsibility is to present the Word of God with every avenue possible at every moment possible to everyone possible, but especially to his children."[12]

I have this vivid image in my mind from my childhood, scores of nearly palpable memories of me coming down the stairs in the morning to find my father in prayer. I can still smell his mug of coffee sitting on the end table. I can hear the pages of his Bible crinkling underneath his folded hands as he knelt in front of that old blue armchair, his face buried in the cushion, lifting up prayers for his family.

That's a Joshua. That's a shepherd leader. That's a husband trying to lead his wife. That's a father trying to disciple his children. And we need more men like this.

I don't say we need more men like this just because of Paul's words in Ephesians 5 and 6. I say we need more men like this simply because they are absent in far too many of the homes in my community and, most likely, your community. Our homes need shepherds. Our homes need pastors. Our homes need men who will lead, love, serve, and disciple.

Our church has a soccer academy for the children of our neighborhood each week. They come to the church house and spend a couple of hours playing soccer. They stretch, run laps, go through drills, scrimmage one another, even learn how to hit the soccer ball with their heads. Oranges are passed out, team pictures are taken each season, and there is a "Living Water Break," allowing them to hydrate while hearing the gospel.

One of the greatest things that takes place at this soccer academy, however, is the relationship between the children and their coaches. You see, the coaches are men from our church. Christian men. Husbands. Fathers. And the majority of the children who spend their Wednesday nights playing soccer with us come from homes lacking a man, much less a God-fearing man. Those Wednesday nights, running around with their coaches, may be the only two hours of their week when they have a Christian man investing in their lives.

And they are desperate for it.

And your home is, too.

The Bible clearly shows the repercussion of the failure of spiritual leadership within the home, whether Adam's failure to lead Eve (Gen. 3) or Ananias failing to lead Saphira (Acts 5). In both cases, sin breaks into the home and, with it, the unwanted feelings of fear, guilt, and shame, along with the unbearable consequences of broken relationship with the Father and physical death.

When spiritual leadership is lacking, someone or something else fills the void. We see this in Genesis 34 when Shechem rapes Jacob's only daughter Dinah. Jacob hears the savage report and, tragically, does nothing. He doesn't yell. He doesn't cry. He doesn't even speak. It's not that he's not an emotional man. Later, when his favorite son, Joseph, is thought to be dead, Jacob tears his clothes, mourns for days, refuses to be comforted, and weeps for his son. With the rape of his daughter, however, he doesn't shed a tear. There is no emotion, no action, and no leadership.

He doesn't say a word and, in the absence of spiritual leadership, someone else will fill the void.

In this case, it is Dinah's brothers, Simeon and Levi, who fill the void by deceiving their sister's offender so that they will be able to easily walk through the city and murder every man. Their genocide goes far beyond an eye-for-an-eye and puts their entire family in danger from the surrounding peoples. Jacob chastises his sons, and yet still refuses to address Dinah's rape. The story ends with Simeon and Levi asking their father, the would-be, should-be spiritual leader of the home, "Should he treat our sister like a prostitute?"

Jacob failed to lead. The sons filled the void, and Jacob rebuked their response. The problem is that he never told them how to respond. He didn't lead them. He didn't guide them through a season of grieving or a plea for justice. He offered no alternative reaction. There was no prayer, no mention of God, and no one to shepherd the family.

The need for spiritual leaders is great. The danger of not having them is disastrous.

Husbands, fathers, can you imagine the transformation that would come to your home if this year found you growing in your spiritual leadership of your wife and children, enjoying the responsibility of pointing them to Christ?

A Word for Wives

My wife, Jessica, has innumerable strengths. She's a creative photographer, a gifted teacher, a wise counselor, a faithful disciple maker, an all-star athlete, a passionate missionary, an extraordinary wife, a remarkable mother, and can cook some Monkey Bread like nobody's business. Jess is funny, brilliant, and stop-traffic gorgeous. She is simply stunning. However, if I'm going to be completely honest, she also has a weakness or two, one of which is her sense of direction. She'd be lost daily without her GPS, and when we're together, she prefers that I drive. Now, I don't always know where I'm going either, but I do enjoy the role of family driver.

It's a small thing, perhaps, but it is a chance to lead, and it's a chance for my wife to let me lead. Leading Jess as we drive, her trusting me, sitting comfortable in the front seat, gives us a small glimpse of what we aim to model in the spiritual aspects of our home. The key, however, is that as I lead, I'm following the map, GPS, and road signs, depending on their guidance. If I begin to ignore the map, GPS, and road signs, making wrong turns, missing exits, and not concerned at all with correcting it, then Jess would be less comfortable trusting me to lead. I can only lead her when I'm following the map, just as spiritual leaders can only lead when following Christ. This we affirmed at the beginning of the chapter.

Now here's my word of encouragement to wives:

When I make a wrong turn, Jess does not immediately kick me out of the driver's seat and take over. She doesn't hit some secret eject button that catapults me through the roof or use a nail gun to fix the map to my forehead. She shows me grace, prays for me, and encourages me to get us back on the right road.

Wives, I don't know your husband or your situation. But I do know that if your husband is to ever lead you spiritually, he's going to desperately need your support, prayers, and encouragement. He's going to need grace. Grace when he fails. Grace when's he's apathetic. Grace when he's lost. Too many husbands have been ejected out of the spiritual leadership seat because they failed years ago, and they have never tried to sit there again.

Wives, are you supporting your husband as the spiritual leader of your home? Are you praying that he will fulfill this role? Are you creating an atmosphere that allows him to feel comfortable stepping up as the Joshua who says, our family will be a Gospel Family? Do you encourage him and pray for him when he fails, or do you criticize and try to take over?

If we are going to see Gospel Families, we are going to have to see Joshuas stand up with the support of the entire home as they intentionally and boldly claim their family for Jesus Christ and his worship.

A Word for Believers with Unbelieving Spouses

A Gospel Family home will always prove challenging. It can be especially difficult, however, if only one of the spouses is fighting for this sort of vision. Some Christian husbands will find themselves trying to lead and shepherd a wife who does not follow after Jesus or share his desire to bring the Gospel into the home. Likewise, some Christian wives will find themselves praying for a home filled with Family Devotions, Family Worship, and Family Missions, while their unbelieving husbands refuse to partner in this journey.

Paul addresses this marital dynamic in his letter to one of the New Testament churches. He calls the Christian spouse to remain married to the unbelieving spouse. He doesn't pretend there won't be challenges. He does, however, encourage a Gospel perspective even in a home where one spouse does not believe the Gospel. Paul writes, "For how do you know, wife, whether you will save your husband? Or how do you know, husband, whether you will save your wife?" (1 Corinthians 7:16).

Peter also views the believing spouse as a missionary in the home, writing, "Likewise, wives, be subject to your own husbands, so that even if some do not obey the word, they may be won without a word by the conduct of their wives, when they see your respectful and pure conduct" (1 Peter 3:1-2).

I have seen a man lead his family, modeling Christ for his home, even when his wife refused to trust Jesus with her life, children, or health. I have seen a woman discipling her children, pointing them to Jesus, even when her husband hid from his responsibility to shepherd the home. One woman in our church prayed for her husband's salvation for more than 20 years. Now, they serve together, as a Christian couple, leading a local missions ministry in our church.

Prayer is powerful, for the one to whom we pray is all powerful. Every family aiming to be a Gospel Family will rest on prayer, and every spouse aiming to shepherd a Gospel home, alongside an unbelieving spouse, can place all of their hopes, needs, prayers, and dependence in Christ. Perhaps the Lord will use you and your prayers to point your spouse to Jesus and his Gospel.

A Word for Single Adults, Single Parents, and Widows

When we consider spiritual leadership and the need for Joshuas, we're not just talking about husbands and wives. What about spiritual leadership in the home of our single adults, our single parents, our widows? The same principle applies: Spiritual leadership is always about recognizing Christ as the head, about submitting to his Lordship, about following him as we lead others.

John Piper defines spiritual leadership as, "Knowing where God wants people to be and taking the initiative to use God's methods to get them there in reliance on God's power."[13]

For the homes without a husband or father, let me suggest three practical applications for spiritual leadership.

1. The spiritual leader of every home, the Shepherd of every home, should be Christ. So whether there's a husband or not, families are to first look toward Jesus for this guidance. Single adults, single moms, widows, and others, can root their homes in the Gospel with healthy, biblical spiritual leadership by simply following Christ as their Shepherd. To the unmarried woman, I would encourage you with the beautiful truth that you are a bride, and that your Bridegroom is Jesus. Allow the Groom to lead your home.

2. If you have others in your home, lead them. I especially want to encourage the single mothers reading right now. Your call to make disciples begins with your children. Invest in their spiritual growth with even more passion and attention than their physical growth. This is done, again, I believe, by following the examples of Joshua: Highlight God's presence, get rid of idols, and worship the Lord. In her book, *The Mission of Motherhood*, Sally Clarkson underlines this call for mothers to model their faith in their home. She writes, "Our children will learn righteousness best by seeing it lived out in every possible way in our lives, moment by moment, in the context of normal life. As I walk honestly before God, with my children watching, they will learn how to have a real relationship with him as well. As they see me apologize to them and pray in front of them to ask for God's forgiveness

in my own life, my children will learn that God is a God of grace who forgives me and guides me."[14]

3. Lean on the extended Gospel Family, the church. Allow the Body of Christ to come alongside you in your pursuit of a gospel-rooted home. Welcome the spiritual leadership of your pastors and elders, and invite them to help disciple your household.

Recently, my family and I needed a vacation. It was late in the year and we had yet to use any vacation days. Ministry at the church was exciting, growing, and busy, and we knew it was time for a Sabbath rest. We prayed for a place to get away, a place where we could enjoy, not just family time, but a retreat of sorts. The Lord opened the door for us to spend a few days at the Jordan Ranch, about an hour and a half west of our city.

The Jordan Ranch began its ministry with a focus on families and has yet to drift from this emphasis. Throughout the year, they invest in families from all over the nation through retreats, counseling, coaching, and through a variety of other ministries. One such ministry is their annual father and son campout. More than 1,000 fathers and sons come to the ranch, set up their tents, and spend the weekend seeking Christ together.

What I love about the campout is the way they reach out to single mothers. They include the children of single moms in the campout as another father spends the retreat with them. This is a beautiful picture of the church, as a brother in Christ partners with his sister in Christ in the discipleship of her children.

This is just one more way family shepherds can point to the Good Shepherd.

I believe the Lord calls the church to love the children of single mothers in a special way. As Dr. James Dobson encourages, "To every single mom who is on this quest, let me emphasize first that you have an invaluable resource in our heavenly Father. He created your children and they are precious to him. How do I know that? Because he said repeatedly in his Word that he has a special tenderness for fatherless children and their mothers. There are many references in Scripture to their plight. For example:

- Deuteronomy 10:17-18: The Lord your God… defends the cause of the fatherless and the widow, and loves the alien, giving him food and clothing.

- Deuteronomy 27:19: Cursed is the man who withholds justice from the alien, the fatherless or the widow.

- Psalm 68:5: A father to the fatherless, a defender of widows, is God in his holy dwelling.

- Zechariah 7:10: Do not oppress the widow or the fatherless, the alien or the poor."[15]

We are all leaders. No matter who you are, if you are a follower of Christ, then you are a spiritual leader of someone else in your life. Someone is looking to you for spiritual leadership, guidance, answers, counsel, encouragement, prayer, and an example. If we're far from Christ, we'll never lead, and if fear trumps faith, we'll never lead. But, if we can trust in Christ while abiding in him, then I believe God will raise up spiritual leaders and shepherds for our homes.

Family Discussion Questions

1. How does your family spend your evenings? Free time? Vacation?

2. According to the way you spend your time, what does your family value the most?

3. If someone who didn't know you watched you and your family for a week, would they say you are a worshiper of Jesus Christ? What would they say you and your family were devoted to primarily?

4. Who is leading your family today?

5. What was the most challenging word from this chapter?

6. Are you a Joshua, leading your family to worship and serve the Lord?

CHAPTER 4

Restoration for the Broken Home

What Broke My Home?

BEFORE WE CAN CONSIDER RESTORATION for our broken homes, we need to ask the question, what broke our homes in the first place? The short answer, often, is sin. However, this might not always be the case, as some families have collapsed into the rubble due to unforeseen economic decline, unemployment, unplanned challenges, or even tragic situations. My prayer for these families is that this chapter would reinforce their hope for a miraculous healing, and that they would find restoration, whatever the source of their brokenness might be.

Other readers will concede that sin was indeed at the root of their family's fall. Whether it was the sin of apathy, adultery, addiction, pride, debt, selfishness, dishonesty, hateful communication, cold disdain, rebellious children, distant husbands, or disrespectful wives, the sin in the home can be as diverse as families themselves.

I want you to think for a moment about what you do when you hear the doorbell. You're in your living room, watching TV, and the doorbell rings. If you're like me, you slowly walk to the door, running every possible scenario through your mind of who might be there. Is it a salesman trying to get me locked into a magazine subscription? Girl Scout with her cookies? Unannounced friend? Neighbor needing to borrow some sugar (do neighbors still do this)? We don't just swing the door open, though, to find out. We use the door's equivalent of caller ID: the peephole. Looking through this small little hole in the door, we check to see who's on the other side wanting to get into our home. Once the identity is revealed, we make a calculated decision to either let them in or pretend we're not home.

When Cain was tempted to kill his brother Abel in Genesis chapter 4, God told Cain that sin was at his doorstep. It was there waiting to devour him, to destroy him. Our doorsteps are no different. Sin is loitering by the front door, waiting to get into our homes. Regrettably, many families spend more time deliberating whether or not to open the door to the Girl Scout than they do deciding whether or not to open the door to sin.

Broken families that point to sin as the root of their past destruction repeatedly remember that they were the ones who opened the door to sin and let it into their living rooms. Fires burn in the corners of our homes, existing as a part of the room, as we ignore them, believing that these small fires, little areas of sin, could never do much harm. When these fires spread and consume everything we've built, we feel surprised, dumbfounded as to how they got there in the first place.

So how does sin enter the home? What really takes place when we open the front door and allow the fires to ignite our rooms and hearts?

In Genesis 3, we see sin enter a family for the first time.

Adam and Eve, the first family, open the door to the sin crouching at the doorstep and the fires burn wildly, destroying the original design.

In this story, sin broke into the home when the family exchanged truth for lies and when they served the creation rather than the Creator.

Satan approaches Eve and begins immediately questioning God's word. Eve responds well at first. But then the serpent goes straight for the heart, calling God a liar. Eve knows what God has said and, therefore, knows that the wages of sin would be death. Satan calls this truth a lie, saying, "You will not die."

This is the lie the family embraces, the crack in the door that allows sin to slither in.

Sin enters the home when we exchange God's truth, his Word, for the lies of the enemy, the world, and the flesh. As Paul writes to the church in Rome, "God gave them up in the lusts of their hearts to impurity, to the dishonoring of their bodies among themselves, because they exchanged the truth about God for a lie" (Romans 1:24-25).

The second crack in the foundation of this first home comes when they choose to serve the creation rather than the Creator.

Adam was to have dominion over creation, over all creatures, over the serpent. But instead, here we find this family submitting to the serpent, giving undeserved attention to creation rather than deserved worship to the Creator.

Eve sees the draw of the world as described in 1 John 2:16: "For all that is in the world—the desires of the flesh and the desires of the eyes and pride of life—is not from the Father but is from the world."

Once again Paul points to this exchange as the slope that brings us into a downward spiral of sin, writing, "God gave them up in the lusts of their hearts to impurity, to the dishonoring of their bodies among themselves, because they exchanged the truth about God for a lie, and worshiped and served the creature rather than the Creator" (Romans 1:24-25).

Adam and Eve adopt the lies of the creature and their family is forever changed. Immediately, fear enters. Guilt enters. Separation from God enters. Shame enters. They try to cover their shame with fig leaves, but the end of the chapter demonstrates that only a sacrifice provided by God can cover our shame. They try to play the blame game as Eve points her finger at the serpent and Adam points his at Eve.

All seems hopeless.

Flames engulf the home and restoration appears impossible. But that's the exact moment when God intervenes.

As soon as sin enters, God unveils His plan for redemption. Genesis 3:15 is called the *protoevangelium*, the first Good News, for this is the first proclamation of the Good News of a coming Redeemer. Once this promise is given, you can almost feel the Biblical narrative waiting for this seed, this descendent of the woman who will come and crush Satan. When Cain and Abel are born, we wonder, will it be Abel? Will it be Seth? Noah? Abraham? Isaac? Jacob? Judah or Joseph? Moses? Joshua? Samuel? David?

Jesus?

Will Jesus be the sacrifice provided by God to cover our shame? Will Jesus be the one who crushes Satan?

1 John 3:8 testifies, that Jesus, the Son of God, is the one we've been expecting: "The reason the Son of God appeared was to destroy the works of the devil."

Hebrews 2:14 agrees: "Since therefore the children share in flesh and blood, he himself likewise partook of the same things, that through death he might destroy the one who has the power of death, that is, the devil."

The consequences of sin in Genesis 3 are shame and death. The punishment for sin is pain for the woman's childbirth and thorns for the ground the man will work. So, in the aftermath of this nuclear attack on the home, we find shame, pain, thorns, and death. We all experience the weight of these, for we are all sinners. But God sent His Son, Jesus Christ to bear the weight of our sin with all of its consequences.

Jesus bore our shame, he endured our pain, he took our thorns, and he died our death.

Because Adam ushered in death, Jesus will bring forth life.

Because Adam broke intimacy with God, Jesus will reconcile sinners to God.

Because Adam ate from the tree, Jesus will hang from the tree.

This is the gospel of reconciliation, the gospel of restoration, the gospel of hope for every family who has opened the door to sin, ignored the fires until the home was consumed, and who reads these words from a place of brokenness.

Out of the Rubble

We all know our homes well. We know where the door is located, how many rooms we have, and which walls have cracks and chipped paint. We know what we like and we know what we would like to change.

Families are a lot like houses. We know our families well, and we know where the cracks are. We know what has caused hurt, what sin has proven destructive, and what we'd like to change. Many of us would like to rebuild our families from scratch, and yet we can't.

At the end of the Sermon on the Mount, Jesus calls his audience to obedience, assuring them that a foundation of God's Word will carry them through the storms of life.

49

Jesus says, "Everyone then who hears these words of mine and does them will be like a wise man who built his house on the rock. And the rain fell, and the floods came, and the winds blew and beat on that house, but it did not fall, because it had been founded on the rock. And everyone who hears these words of mine and does not do them will be like a foolish man who built his house on the sand. And the rain fell, and the floods came, and the winds blew and beat against that house, and it fell, and great was the fall of it" (Matthew 7:24-27).

Unfortunately, many homes today have experienced the fate of the foolish man. Unfortunately, many homes today have come crashing down because God's Word was not the foundation of the home. Many families have fallen greatly because Family Discipleship, Family Worship, and Family Missions had no place in their home. Some of you are reading this from a place of brokenness, from the rubble of a fallen home.

When my wife and I bought our first house, I learned that we had to have an inspection done before we could close on the house. We paid an inspector to come out, look all through the house, climb into the attic, and examine the foundation. Afterwards, he gave us a booklet of pictures and notes, detailing every imperfection of the home. It was informative, to be sure. But then, the inspector left. That's it. No solution, no repairs, just a list of problems.

Anyone can inspect a home or a family and give a list of all of the unhealthy spots, all of the broken places, and then walk away. We're not called to be inspectors who turn over the rocks to expose the dirt beneath, only to walk away shaking our heads. We're called to be light to the darkness, allowing Christ to work through us to restore the brokenness.

So what do we do if we are sitting in the rubble? What do we do if the storms have already destroyed our family?

How can a broken home be rebuilt?
How can a hurting family be restored?

¡Creyendo lo Imposible!

Let us begin by rejoicing in the truth that the Lord can heal, the Lord can comfort, the Lord can restore!

Many doubt this. Many people sit in my office, sharing the wounds of their families, describing in detail just how shattered their homes have become and just how deep the cracks run. Then they tell me that nothing will ever change.

I've learned that our first move toward any hope of restoration is to establish hope, for I've learned that many of these families have no hope.

My first missions experience outside of the States took place in Morelos, Mexico, soon after I gave my life to Christ. Morelos is a little pueblo just a couple of hours past the border of Mexico and Texas. We spent that week serving with a pastor and his church, Rodolfo Gomez. The Lord quickly united my heart with his as I was inspired by his love for his people, his gracious heart, and his vision for the community. Over the years, the Lord has opened up the door for me to serve with Pastor Rodolfo (Fito) several times, including a four-month season, during which my friend and I lived with Fito and his family.

Those months in Mexico were some of my favorite times of ministry, and it wasn't just because we ate migas every morning for breakfast. I enjoyed sharing life with this pastor and his family, took advantage of the opportunity to learn a little Spanish, appreciated the weekly soccer games that gave me the chance to make a fool of myself, and I delighted in the afternoon siestas. I fell in love with the people and the culture, as well as the Lord's mission for the nations.

Fito's church that welcomed us so warmly had a mission statement: "Creyendo lo Imposible," meaning, "Believing the

Impossible." Simple. Faithful. Impactful. When Fito would counsel families who had given up on their marriage or the Lord's ability to restore the home, he would call them back to the mission to be a people who believe the impossible.

If we are going to be a people who believe in Jesus, his death and resurrection, then we are to be a people who believe the impossible. If we believe that Jesus rose from the dead, why do we not believe he can raise our families up from the dead? Why do we not believe he can pull us out of the rubble and restore and heal?

It's absurd to believe in the resurrection of Christ and simultaneously doubt his ability to restore our families.

Our church sings a worship song that combines these two ideas. It's a praise song by Israel And New Breed, called, "Rez Power." One of the verses declares, the hope the broken have in Christ as well as the power of Christ to overcome the grave. How appropriate to simultaneously proclaim our hope for broken hearts while proclaiming Jesus' victory over the grave, for it is his life, his powerful resurrection, that allows dead hearts, wounded families, and shattered homes to hope for the impossible.

As we see in Scripture, "He heals the brokenhearted and binds up their wounds" (Psalm 147:3).

Examples of Restoration

Let's look at two stories of restoration in the home:

Luke 15:11-24—And he said, "There was a man who had two sons. And the younger of them said to his father, 'Father, give me the share of property that is coming to me.' And he divided his property between them. Not many days later, the younger son gathered all he had and took a journey into a far country, and there he squandered his property in reckless living.

And when he had spent everything, a severe famine arose in that country, and he began to be in need. So he went and hired himself out to one of the citizens of that country, who sent him into his fields to feed pigs. And he was longing to be fed with the pods that the pigs ate, and no one gave him anything.

"But when he came to himself, he said, 'How many of my father's hired servants have more than enough bread, but I perish here with hunger! I will arise and go to my father, and I will say to him, "Father, I have sinned against heaven and before you. I am no longer worthy to be called your son. Treat me as one of your hired servants."' And he arose and came to his father. But while he was still a long way off, his father saw him and felt compassion, and ran and embraced him and kissed him.

"And the son said to him, 'Father, I have sinned against heaven and before you. I am no longer worthy to be called your son.'

But the father said to his servants, 'Bring quickly the best robe, and put it on him, and put a ring on his hand, and shoes on his feet. And bring the fattened calf and kill it, and let us eat and celebrate. For this my son was dead, and is alive again; he was lost, and is found.'

And they began to celebrate."

How was restoration found in this home, for this family?

Most significantly, there was repentance. There was a genuine turning from the sinful path back to the path that leads to the father.

Also, there was forgiveness. The father, wounded, taken advantage of, with reason to be angry, chose to forgive his son. Instead of closed doors he found open arms. In the place of a cold welcome, he was extended a warm meal. Rather than demanding an explanation, the father ordered a party.

If broken homes are to be restored, we must follow this example and celebrate repentance and forgiveness.

Another Biblical example of this sort of restoration comes just four chapters later:

> **Luke 19:1-10**—He entered Jericho and was passing through. And behold, there was a man named Zacchaeus. He was a chief tax collector and was rich. And he was seeking to see who Jesus was, but on account of the crowd he could not, because he was small in stature. So he ran on ahead and climbed up into a sycamore tree to see him, for he was about to pass that way.
>
> And when Jesus came to the place, he looked up and said to him, "Zacchaeus, hurry and come down, for I must stay at your house today." So he hurried and came down and received him joyfully.
>
> And when they saw it, they all grumbled, "He has gone in to be the guest of a man who is a sinner."
>
> And Zacchaeus stood and said to the Lord, "Behold, Lord, the half of my goods I give to the poor. And if I have defrauded anyone of anything, I restore it fourfold."
>
> And Jesus said to him, "Today salvation has come to this house, since he also is a son of Abraham. For the Son of Man came to seek and to save the lost."

How was restoration found in this home, for this family?

The head of the household sought Jesus.

The head of the household welcomed Jesus into his home.

The head of the household repented of his sin and made things right with those he had wronged.

The head of the household found forgiveness and salvation in Jesus Christ who actively seeks and saves the lost.

Tackling the issue of spiritual leadership, I wrote, we need more Joshuas. Now, as we set our hearts on restoration, let me say, we need more leaders like Zacchaeus. We need heads of homes that will seek Jesus, welcome him into their family situations, repent of sin, and find the freedom of forgiveness. This is how shattered foundations are made new.

Draw Near to the Restorer of Families

There's a mall close to our house that my kids love. They love it because there's a beautiful, two-story carousel in the food court. When my daughter, Gracie, was younger, she would only ride the zebra, so this mall is affectionately known in our home as the "Zebra Mall." Nowadays, however, she prefers the tea cup ride, leaving my wife and me to engage in a friendly "rock, paper, scissors" to see who has to ride the spiniest, dizziest ride on the carousel, certain to make us throw up or pass out. Accompanying my son Silas on the tiger that slowly moves up and down proves much easier and much less nauseating.

Not too long ago, we had spent all of our carousel tokens and were ready to leave. Since it was raining outside, my wife and kids waited by the front door while I ran through the parking lot to get the car. Two minutes later, I pulled around to pick them up only to find my two-year-old son bleeding and crying. I wish I could say my family just falls apart when I'm not there, but the truth is these sorts of injuries usually happen on my watch.

Apparently Silas was spinning around in circles while they waited for me to get the car. Jess kept telling him to stay close to her, but he spun further and further away until, finally, and perhaps, inevitably, he crashed his head into the sharp corner of a metal pole. He hit it hard and fell harder. Zebra Mall had become Bloody Head Wound Mall.

Crashes and falls come when we spin further and further away from the Lord. He calls us to draw near, to abide in him, to rest in him, to follow him, but we just keep spinning and spinning further and further away from the presence of Christ until we eventually plow into the sharp, painful consequences of our rebellion, wrecking it all.

Enough spinning. Enough drifting. It's time to draw near. It's time to draw near to the one who can heal, comfort, forgive, and restore. There is hope for every broken home; hope for the impossible; hope for the families who have opened the door to sin, and hope for the family who lives in the debris of the wreckage. There is hope that can be found today. And that hope is in Christ.

Family Discussion Questions

1. What areas of your family need healing?

2. What do you or what does your family need to repent of in order to enjoy true forgiveness?

3. How can you seek Jesus as a family?

4. How can you welcome Jesus into your home?

5. Do you believe that the Lord who seeks and saves and comforts and restores can transform and restore your family?

PART TWO

Cultivating Family Discipleship

CHAPTER 5

Great Commandment Families

A Remarkable Calling

I COULDN'T BELIEVE THE DOCTORS were letting us leave. Our baby was just a few days old, I knew nothing about parenting, and there we were, trying to buckle this 7-pound baby girl into a car seat and no one was there to stop us. We pulled out of the parking lot and were completely on our own. I kept checking my rear view mirror, thinking I'd see an army of nurses chasing after us, yelling, "You can't leave yet! You're not ready! You don't know what you're doing!"

At home, the reality of parenting became even more overwhelming as I realized that our baby girl depended on us for everything. All of her needs rested on us: food, sleep, clothes, baths, clean diapers, and warm blankets. Her beautiful blue eyes would look to us when she needed to be rocked, swaddled, or entertained.

As we've matured in our parenting over the years, however, we've realized that the physical needs of our children are not the most vital. Our most impactful decisions are not whether or not they take their vitamins or wear suntan lotion at the swimming pool. Instead, it is the spiritual, the eternal matters that direct our hearts and prayers for our children.

The greatest call we have as families, is not to take care of one another or provide for one another, but it is to disciple one another. It's a remarkable calling, a joyful responsibility.

Childhood Faith

The joyful responsibility of making disciples within our homes is beautifully reflected in the home of one of the New Testament missionaries, Timothy. As we strive to cultivate Family Discipleship, we would do well to observe the impact Timothy's family had on his spiritual walk.

In Paul's second letter to young Timothy, Paul writes, "I am reminded of your sincere faith, a faith that dwelt first in your grandmother Lois and your mother Eunice and now, I am sure, dwells in you as well" (2 Timothy 1:5).

Even though Paul refers to Timothy as his beloved child, Paul did not first lead Timothy to Christ. Paul was not the first one to open his heart to the Scriptures or to disciple this young pastor.

Timothy's discipleship began in the home.

Timothy was a third generation God-fearer. Faith dwelt in his grandmother, Lois. Faith dwelt in his mother, Eunice. And, because of their Family Discipleship, it was a faith that dwelt in Timothy as well. Paul's discipleship of Timothy, then, is a mere continuation of what his family had already begun. It is an extension of a childhood faith he had always known.

In chapter 3 of the same letter, Paul exhorts Timothy, "Continue in what you have learned and have firmly believed, knowing from whom you learned it and how from childhood you have been acquainted with the sacred writings, which are able to make you wise for salvation through faith in Christ Jesus" (2 Timothy 3:14-15).

His discipleship rested in the Scriptures. From childhood Timothy was familiar with the Word of God that pointed him to faith in Jesus. Let this serve as our maxim for cultivating Family Discipleship: Family Discipleship celebrates God's Word that leads our family to salvation through faith in Jesus Christ.

Any fruitful discipleship embraces a call to obedience (*see Matthew 28:20; Romans 1:5*), and any celebration of God's Word embraces a call to obey the two Great Commandments.

The Greatest Great Commandment

In chapter 1, we looked at the biblical call for spiritual growth in the home: "These words that I command you today shall be on your heart. You shall teach them diligently to your children, and shall talk of them when you sit in your house, and when you walk by the way, and when you lie down, and when you rise. You shall bind them as a sign on your hand, and they shall be as frontlets between your eyes. You shall write them on the doorposts of your house and your gates" (Deuteronomy 6:6-9).

To truly appreciate the might of these verses, we have to meditate on the spark behind these fiery words.

We see it in verse five, for this foundation for Family Discipleship is preceded by the greatest commandment ever given in Scripture: "You shall love the Lord your God with all your heart and with all your soul and with all your might" (Deuteronomy 6:5).

The heart of Family Discipleship is the great commandment, for only families who love the Lord with all of their heart will make disciples who will do the same. If we are to cultivate Family Discipleship in the home, we are going to have to become Great Commandment Families who love the Lord with all of our affections and reproduce this love in others.

Jesus quoted this charge to love God when he was asked to cite the greatest commandment of God's Law. Just before this response, however, Matthew 22 records two other questions brought before Jesus.

First, a group called the Pharisees asked Jesus about taxes. Jesus used this opportunity to remind them that whatever bears the image of Caesar, like man-made coins, belongs to Caesar. Cleverly, however, while the crowds are thinking about Caesar, Jesus emphasizes a much more remarkable truth about God: Whoever bears his image belongs to him. As Jesus said, "Render to Caesar the things that are Caesar's, and to God the things that are God's" (Matthew 22:21).

Secondly, a group called the Sadducees asked Jesus about the resurrection, for they did not believe in any sort of resurrection. In his response, Jesus revealed another significant truth about God: God is the God of the living.

People, bearing the image of God, belong to God, who is the God of the living. Right after these two weighty theological truths are proclaimed, a lawyer from among the Pharisees approaches Jesus with a third question: "Which is the greatest commandment of the Law?"

It is in this context, with God's sovereignty over his image-bearers and his Lordship over the living at the forefront of every mind, that Jesus calls the people to love this awesome Lord with all their heart, soul, and mind.

Just as every family will have a leader, someone or something they follow, someone or something captivates the heart of every family. If our affections are not devoted to God, if our deepest love is not reserved for the Lord, then we will pour these affections out somewhere else.

A Great Commandment family is not just a family who loves. It is a family who loves God with all they are, something that is only possible when we experience all of God's love.

To Know God is to Know Love

Before we can understand how to love God, we must savor God's love. As 1 John 4:19 reads, "We love, because he first loved us." True love, like the kind Jesus speaks about in the Great Commandment, stems out of the rich soil of God's love, so that all of the fruit it produces will reflect his character and nature.

J.I. Packer beautifully describes God's love, writing, "His love finds expression in everything that he says and does."[16]

So, how does God manifest his love toward us? John 3:16 teaches that God demonstrates his love for the world by giving, "his only begotten Son, that whoever believes in him shall not perish, but have eternal life." Paul highlights this glorious truth writing, "God demonstrates his own love toward us, in that while we were yet sinners, Christ died for us" (Romans 5:8). He died on the cross so that we may be adopted into his family.

As Packer summarizes, "The New Testament gives us two yardsticks for measuring God's love. The first is the cross; the second is the gift of sonship."[17]

John also reminds the church of this love in his letters:

1 John 4:9—By this the love of God was manifested in us, that God has sent his only begotten Son into the world so that we might live through him.

1 John 3:16—We know love by this, that he laid down his life for us; and we ought to lay down our lives for the brethren.

D.A. Carson notes, "God's love is both the model and the incentive of our love."[18]

We can begin to teach this in our homes even when our children are young. We can apply the deep love of Christ to their hearts from the earliest of ages. I see this possibility every time I sing *Jesus Loves Me* with my 2-year-old son Silas.

When we get to the chorus he always sings loud. Lying there in his bed he cries out, "*Yes, Jesus loves Silas, Yes, Jesus loves Silas, Yes, Jesus loves Silas, the Bible tells me so.*"

All on his own, he has found a way to personalize the love of Christ. All on his own, he has found a way to rejoice over the love that Jesus has for him. All on his own, through a simple song, Silas is already coming to know, little by little, the love of Christ.

This matters, because apart from knowing the love of Christ, we cannot love at all. We can offer, at best, the fallen world's version of love: twisted, incomplete, perverted, selfish, unsatisfying versions of God's love.

Can a family devoid of the love of Christ love the Lord, or even each other, for that matter? Absolutely not. God is love. He's not just our best example of love. He's not just loving. He is Love. Apart from God, there is no love. Absent of Christ in our lives, there is no love. There is a world's imitation of love, filled with emotion and sentiment and commitments driven by the flesh and relationships founded upon natural feelings, but there is no love—not in the true, genuine, full sense.

Our best effort at loving someone else is still but a mere glimpse into what Christ offers all who abide in him. As Spurgeon wrote, "Sweet above all other things is love—a mother's love, a father's love, a husband's love, a wife's love—but all these are only faint images of the love of God."[19]

How do we know if we love Jesus with this sort of love? Jesus says those who love him obey his commandments:

- John 14:15—If you love me, you will keep my commandments.

- John 15:10—If you keep my commandments, you will abide in my love.

Abiding in Christ, we are filled with an indescribable,

unconditional love that is to then overflow out of us in our love to God, painting a picture of a Great Commandment family.

If we neglect this first commandment, we'll have no hope in keeping the second commandment.

The Second Greatest Great Commandment

Jesus continues his response to the lawyer, saying, the second greatest commandment is to love your neighbor as yourself. We are not called to just model godly love in our devotion to the Lord. As our families abide in Christ and love God, we are to reproduce this love in our neighbors.

- 1 John 4:21— And this commandment we have from Him, that the one who loves God should love his brother also.

- John 13:35—By this all men will know that you are my disciples, if you have love for one another.

Families who keep these two commandments keep the law to the glory of Christ. This is the theme traced throughout the Bible, accented by Paul:

He who loves his neighbor has fulfilled the law…if there is any other commandment, it is summed up in this saying, "You shall love your neighbor as yourself." Love does no wrong to a neighbor; therefore love is the fulfillment of the law (Romans 13:8-10).

If we neglect this second commandment we prove that we have neglected the first commandment.

- 1 John 3:17—Whoever has the world's goods, and sees his brother in need and closes his heart against him, how does the love of God abide in him?

- 1 John 4:8—The one who does not love does not know God, for God is love.

- 1 John 4:11—Beloved, if God so loved us, we also ought to love one another.

- 1 John 4:12—If we love one another, God abides in us and his love is perfected in us.

- 1 John 4:20—If someone says, "I love God," and hates his brother, he is a liar; for the one who does not love his brother whom he has seen, cannot love God whom he has not seen.

My wife is truly gifted in teaching our children the Word of God. She organically incorporates family devotions into their morning routine, engages them in spiritual conversations in the car, sings worship songs as she rocks them to sleep, and makes Bible crafts each week, like the memory verse monster (a Kleenex box decorated like a monster who eats Bible memory verses as they say them).

One of my favorite ways she's led them to enjoy Christ and his Word during the day is in teaching them their mission. Whenever they are leaving the house to walk to the park, go to the store, or drive to the library, she'll ask our kids, "What's our mission?" They all shout out, "Love people." When I get home from work, the oldest two will often tell me stories of how they "loved people" that day while shopping for bananas and juice packs.

Great Commandment families who abide in the love of Christ will love their neighbors. As many have said, "Know love, show love." Not every family does this. Not every family invests in others. Not every family seeks ways to pour into their neighbors and the least of these. This is a high calling, a difficult command that I know I struggle with daily.

Loving our neighbors requires time, sacrifice, interruption, and inconvenience. The Good Samaritan parable is not a story of convenient service; it's a story of a man going out of his way, allowing his schedule to be interrupted and his finances drained, expending his energy, going above and beyond in order to meet the needs of a complete stranger.

I still remember one of the first times I reached out to love someone. I was in first grade. She was in second grade. We went to church together and I was convinced we needed to be together. So, I did what any man would do. I wrote her a note. My older brother (3rd grade) and his friend (also 3rd grade) helped me craft this legendary love letter. It rivaled Shakespeare:

I love you. Do you love me? Check the box: ❑ *Yes or* ❑ *No*

At the last minute, my brother suggested I add a third box. After all, love is tricky; complicated even. So, we allowed one more edit:

I love you. Do you love me? Check the box: ❑ *Yes or* ❑ *No or* ❑ *So-So*

Brilliant!

We had our church sign-language class that evening, affording me the perfect opportunity to boldly declare my love, by having my friend deliver the note secretly. She spent a few minutes reading the letter and making a few notes of her own, before her messenger returned it to my messenger, who delivered the heartbreaking news to me. She had added a 4th box:

Check the box: ❑ *Yes or* ❑ *No or* ❑ *So-So* ☑ *In God's Way*

Not only did she crush my heart with the 4th box, she scribbled a little piece of advice at the bottom of the letter. The 2nd grader told me, the 1st grader, to ask someone my "own age." That was the night I learned sign language for, "humiliated."

Everyone we encounter could be seen as giving us a letter, asking us to check the box that defines our love for him or her. How often do we check, "No"? How often do we add another box? We add boxes that justify and excuse. We add boxes that say, "Yes, but I'm a bit too busy today." Boxes that read, "Yes, but it would be best if you came back another day." Do we send them away with a piece of advice to ask someone else? How often do our families check the "Yes" box and then prove it by our actions?

Gospel Families are Great Commandment Families, enjoying the love of Christ in such a powerful way that they naturally and joyfully love the Lord and those around them, ceaselessly checking, "Yes," and ceaselessly proving we mean it.

Family Discussion Questions

1. What competes for our love, making it hard to love God with all of our heart?

2. Who is the neighbor that we are to love?

3. How can we, as a family, love people?

4. What are some practical ways our neighbors and friends see the love of Christ in our homes?

5. Do our relationships, attitudes, and conversations reflect the Lord's love?

CHAPTER 6

Family Devotions

Is the Gospel for the Whole Family?

I'VE HEARD MY FAIR SHARE of sermons in my life. My dad's a preacher. I'm a preacher, and between Sunday mornings, Sunday evenings, Wednesday evenings, VBS, youth camps, Disciple Now weekends, winter retreats, mission trips, small groups, home groups, life groups, cell groups, house church meetings, seminary chapel, revivals, radio, and, of course, even a few TV evangelists, I've probably heard 9,362 sermons (rough estimate).

Some sermons have been life impacting, while others, forgettable. But there's one sermon I keep coming back to: Peter's sermon from Acts 2.

He sort of hits it all. He walks through the Old Testament, quoting prophecy by memory, before proclaiming the sovereignty of the Father in the crucifixion of Jesus Christ. He preaches the death and resurrection of Jesus, claiming to be a witness of both. Then, he drives it home, saying, "God has made him both Lord and Christ, this Jesus whom you crucified."

"...whom *you* crucified."

Now that's an invitation, call-to-response, pierce-the-heart conclusion if I've ever heard one. The crowd was cut to the heart and asked, "What shall we do?" And I love Peter's answer: "Repent and be baptized every one of you in the name of Jesus Christ for the forgiveness of your sins, and you will receive the gift of the Holy Spirit."

Filled with the Holy Spirit, preaching that Joel's prophecy of the pouring out of the Spirit is being fulfilled in front of their very eyes, Peter now says that they too can receive the gift of the Holy Spirit. But he doesn't stop there.

And this is where Easter weekend breaks through your front door and sits down in the living room with your family.

Peter says that this promised gift of the Holy Spirit is "for you and for your children and for all who are far off, everyone whom the Lord our God calls to himself."

"...and for your children..."

He preaches the death and resurrection of Christ, calls the sinful crowd to repentance for the forgiveness of sins, and then tells them this is also for their children. And I believe it's for our children today as well.

I believe that the bloodstained cross and empty tomb is kid friendly; safe for the whole family.

I believe we should be Acts 2 families. I believe we should realize that the Easter message of the death and resurrection of Christ is for our children. I believe we should preach repentance and the forgiveness of sins in our homes, and I believe we should pray that our entire family would receive the promised gift of the Holy Spirit.

This idea of bringing the Gospel into our home and making it available and clear and impactful for the entire family will require us to begin celebrating Family Discipleship. And, if we are to be found faithful in Family Discipleship, I believe we would be blessed to have a consistent time of prayer, worship, and Scripture reading with our family members.

Cue family devotions.

Implementing Regular Times of Family Devotions

The idea of family devotions can seem quite overwhelming to those who have never had a consistent time of prayer and Gospel celebration in the home. It might seem beyond your family's grasp; something that other families may try, but not yours.

I used to have this image of family devotions, this picture in my head of what it would look like for my family.

There we were, my wife, my four-year-old daughter, my two-year-old son, our newborn boy, and me, all sitting around the dinner table. The table was set, the Bible open, and our hearts ready to approach the Lord together as a family. Music softly played in the background. Everyone was formally dressed, and in a sweet mood with smiles on their faces. I would teach from the Bible, and we would graciously take turns talking while the others quietly chewed their food.

There would be singing (on key) praying (with eyes closed) and spiritual discussion (at a reasonable volume).

I thought it would be this way.

And then, my wife and I had children. We started these family devotions at dinnertime, and all of my dreams of quiet, picture-perfect family devotions evaporated.

Our family devotions are messy. Milk is spilt while I'm reading God's Word, my wife has to get up from the table multiple times to wait on our children, the kids aren't looking for a "quiet time" and usually share their thoughts about the devotion with great emotion, gestures, and noise. They dance and run around the room while we sing praise songs and my son punctuates every prayer with a loud shout of, "Amen!"

But we do approach God as a family. We do worship him

together. We do adore him through Scripture, entreat him through prayer, and exalt him through praise. We just do it while spitting out food we don't like and crying for dessert.

Implementing regular times of family devotions might be messy and, at first, even awkward, but, they will inevitably become more natural over time.

The Purpose of Family Devotions

Family devotions are challenging. They're tough. They require time, commitment, consistency, and patience. It's opening the Bible instead of turning on the TV. It's praying for forgiveness with your children five minutes after yelling at them. It's leading your family at the end of an exhausting day. It's trying different ways of implementing devotions until you find what works for your family.

But family devotions are also rewarding. It's hearing your spouse talk about Jesus with your children. It's catching a glimpse of your daughter's heart as she prays to her Savior. It's your son knowing the story of the cross. It's your family being familiar and comfortable with words like *forgiveness* and *grace*. It's dinnertime Bible studies, living room worship, car ride conversations, and bedtime prayers.

Regardless of the age, background, or personality of those in your home, it is never too early to begin family devotions. As C.H. Spurgeon reminds us, we are to "Begin early to teach, for children begin early to sin."[20]

We see just how rewarding and just how fruitful family devotions can be when we peak through the windows of Timothy's home again, as we did in chapter five.

When we first see Paul meeting Timothy, we learn three things about Timothy: he is a disciple, his mom is a believer, and he is well spoken of by the church (Acts 16:1-2).

Timothy's discipleship began in the home. It was Timothy's grandmother, Lois and his mother, Eunice, who invested in his spiritual walk and spiritual growth. The faith first dwelt in these ladies and was passed down through Family Discipleship to the young man.

I imagine that for these two women, this task of teaching Timothy proved exhausting at times. I imagine there were times when they didn't feel like modeling their faith or encouraging his. And yet they did. And because they did, they saw Timothy grow into an example in speech, conduct, love, faith, and purity. As a result of their discipleship, Timothy was saved and sanctified (2 Timothy 3:15).

This is the purpose of Family Discipleship; namely, the salvation and sanctification of our family.

Family Discipleship is overwhelmingly challenging, but the life-changing fruit that is produced when the home is rooted in the Gospel overshadows the challenges.

One Thing Every Home Needs

Jungle life is unique. Therefore, packing for a trip into the jungle is quite different from any other travel. When I lived in the Amazon as a missionary, I learned how to prepare for two months in an indigenous village. If I was only going to have one backpack, I wanted to make sure that my backpack had everything I needed and nothing I didn't.

There are certain jungle backpack essentials that you'd do well to remember when packing your pack. Here's my top 10 list (not in any particular order): (1) Toilet paper; (2) First aid kit; (3) Purification tablets for the water; (4) Matches; (5) GPS; (6) Mosquito net; (7) Water bottle; (8) Bible & journal; (9) Sleeping bag; (10) Headlamp or flashlight.

I can honestly say that I used all of these just about everyday we spent in the jungle. The headlamp was particularly helpful. Out there, one would rarely leave their hut or tent at nighttime without some sort of flashlight, much less walk down the narrow paths of the rainforest in the dark. A headlamp would allow me to see where I was going while keeping my hands free. The light swivels with your head so that everywhere you look, you see the light and everywhere you turn, the light exposes the dangers, open paths, and closed paths, directing you where to walk, illuminating how to walk.

Everyone in the jungle needs a light that swivels as we turn, always guiding, always protecting, always lighting the way.

I'm sure we could come up with another top 10 list for the home, the essentials, without which, no household could survive. Rather than exploring a long list, however, let's just cut to the chase and focus on the one, most significant thing every home needs: The Light of the Gospel revealed through the Word of God.

This is more powerful and much more necessary than a headlamp, for the risk of leaving it out of our family's backpack and the blessing of packing it first are far greater than what is experienced with a jungle flashlight.

Our homes are filled with furniture, appliances, entertainment, clothes, toys, pictures, people, memories, dreams, failures, needs, regrets, and hopes. In the midst of it all, though, do we have a guiding light? Are we devoted to the Word of God in such a way that it is like a light on our foreheads, illuminating all that is in our path, whichever way we turn?

Family devotions, regular times of praying together and delighting in the Scriptures with one another, will bless your home with this light.

Just days before I married my wife, Jess, one of my dear friends told me, "Families that pray together, stay together." This was not, necessarily, the deepest, most profound, theological marriage counsel I received from friends or books, but they have proven to be some of the most true and most important. Jess and I took these words to heart and spent time every morning in prayer with one another. She would share her heart, praises, and needs, and I would do the same before we entered into the presence of the Lord together in prayer. These were our first expressions of family devotions, and these sweet, quiet times of prayer in the early hours strengthened the foundation of our marriage unlike anything else.

Whether it's a consistent morning of prayer, sweet time of worship, or purposeful moments of enjoying the Scriptures, family devotions are the bedrock of a Gospel Family.

3 Ways to Make the Gospel Relevant to your Family

Many articles and books have been published recently about making the Gospel relevant. The heart behind it all, I believe, is to find a way to take a message written 2000 years ago about events that took place 2000 years ago on the other side of the world, and make it relate to families today. The premise, I assume, is that it is challenging to apply words from the Bible to the modern family of 2014.

While I understand the challenge of communicating the story of Jesus to different generations, cultures, and families, I don't believe that the Gospel message needs much help in becoming relevant, for as I read the words of Scripture, it seems to cut to the heart all on its own.

So here are three things I think we can do to make the Gospel relevant in the home today as we teach the Word of God during our family devotions:

1. **Preach the Gospel:** Many people can't relate to the Gospel because it has been altered, confused, and watered-down. The power is lost. The message is unclear, and the impact, weak. Instead, let us share the Gospel message exactly how the early church shared it. Paul reminds the church of the Gospel saying, simply, "that Christ died for our sins, he

was buried, and he was raised on the third day" (1 Corinthians 15:3-4). The power of the Gospel is not found in the creative delivery of the sermon or in the modern illustrations and references that make it more accessible. The Gospel is powerful in and of itself. As Paul writes, "I am not ashamed of the gospel, for it is the power of God for salvation to everyone who believes" (Romans 1:16). If we long to see our families today understand and believe the Gospel, let us simply preach the Gospel, boldly, clearly, so that, as with Peter's audience hearing the preaching of the Gospel (Acts 2:37), our families today will be cut to the heart, repent, and put their faith in Jesus for the forgiveness of their sins.

2. **Live the Gospel:** One of the most powerful testimonies comes when the lost world encounters a faithful family. Any culture of any generation can relate to a message that claims to change lives when they see that it has actually changed lives. Transformation is relevant. Hope is relevant. Joy is relevant. Peace is relevant. Forgiveness is relevant, for everyone talks of these things, longs for these things, and is searching for these things. I believe they will find it in the Gospel when they find it alive in our homes. When they see what they've heard, when we live what we've declared, modern culture will worship the Marvelous Christ. Like the unbeliever of 1 Corinthians 14:24 who hears the prophesy of the church and falls on his face to worship God, and like the suicidal jailer of Acts 16 who believes in Jesus after witnessing missionaries worship Christ in the midst of persecution, today's families will worship and believe as they

encounter, not just the Gospel, but a living Gospel overflowing out of our homes.

3. **Listen:** Far too often, we preach and live the Gospel, but we fail to do these in the context of relationships and meaningful conversations. Those who aim to see the Gospel relevant today should begin by listening. Listen to the heart of your spouse and children. Listen to their journeys. Hear their stories. Discern where they are, and begin there. Philip witnessed to the man from Ethiopia by explaining Scripture from the Old Testament book of Isaiah (Acts 8). Peter witnessed to Cornelius by telling the story of Jesus' life, death and resurrection, beginning with his baptism (Acts 10). Paul witnessed to the city of Athens by proclaiming the "unknown God" and his creation (Acts 17). They all preached and lived the same Gospel. They all pointed the lost to Jesus Christ. But they also listened. They observed. Philip stood by the chariot and listened to what the Ethiopian man was reading. Peter asked Cornelius to first share his story, and Paul spent days examining the idolatry of the city before addressing the Areopagus. Our families don't need us to be entertaining or funny or worldly, but I do believe they need us to listen, and then share the Good News of Christ so that it penetrates their hearts and meets them where they are, which is what the Gospel always does. It is relevant because it does meet us where we are. It meets a sinful person with forgiveness, a wicked person with a new heart, the depressed with comfort, the anxious with peace, the hateful with love. And the Gospel meets the dead person with life (Ephesians 2:1-10).

4 Ways to Cultivate Family Devotions

1. Establish a regular time and place for your family devotions. Whether you sit down with your family at the table every night and pray and read the Word of God together over dinner, or make it a Saturday morning tradition, it is important that your family grows to expect and even look forward to these memorable times of Family Devotions.

2. Buy a Family Devotion book. If you have children, you can purchase a children's Bible that will help you disciple them and teach them the Word of God. There are devotionals for married couples, engaged couples, singles, the new believer, and the mature believer. These resources can help you practice and strengthen spiritual disciplines like Bible study, prayer, and worship as you seek ways to further enjoy the presence of Christ. Our ministry posts free family devotions on our website: www. GospelFamily.org. We also have a free book on iBooks entitled: 31 Days of Praying Scripture Over Your Family.

3. Order the International Mission Board's West Africa Storying Cloth (http://imbresources.org/index.cfm/product/detail/prodID/1619). This is a beautifully designed cloth with 42 pictures of 42 different Bible stories, presented in chronological order. It comes with the accompanying Scriptures, equipping you to walk your family through the Bible over the course of a year. You can hang it on the wall and review the previous stories each time you introduce a new one. There are other chronological Bible story resources available online that will help you think through common

threads found in the stories as well as application questions to ask your family after each story.

4. Develop a regular time of sharing prayer requests with one another. Ask about joys and challenges in each other's lives and then pray together. Pray for provision, protection, purity, wisdom, forgiveness, and spiritual maturity.

Family Discussion Questions

1. What are three goals you can set in order to see family devotions become more evident in your family and home?

2. What is your prayer for your family devotion time?

3. What challenges do you expect to encounter as you try to implement regular times of family devotion?

4. What will help you overcome these challenges?

CHAPTER 7

Praying with and for your Family

Family Prayer Blessings

LET ME SHARE WITH YOU one of the most embarrassing moments of my life.

I was in first grade and I didn't have any friends. My brother had a bunch of friends; even best friends. But my parents worried that I didn't really have any friends that I would consider "close." So, my parents, concerned, called me to their bedroom one evening and had me sit on the floor with them. They made me hold their hands as they prayed for me. They prayed, out loud, with me just sitting there, that the Lord would give me a friend. Can you believe this? Can you picture it? They didn't even pray for *friends* (plural), but for a *friend* (singular). How embarrassing! Humiliated, I left with the bar set pretty low—one friend—but their prayer invoked, nonetheless.

Here's the kicker, though: God answered their prayer. Soon after that appalling prayer, the Lord gave me a best friend and then even some bonus friends after that.

While I might not have felt a spirit of gratitude at the time, I am grateful for parents who prayed with me and for me. I am thankful to have had a family that would take our needs to Jesus in prayer, interceding for one another, trusting God to provide and move and answer, while also giving him all of the praise for every answered prayer.

Just as I affirmed the blessing of praying with my wife in the previous chapter, I have also seen the value of family prayer, now that our family has grown. We pray before meals. We pray when we recognize needs in our home. We pray during our family devotions. We pray before bed, and I often even return to my children's bedrooms after they are asleep so that I may pray over them while they are sleeping.

Regardless of your family dynamic, regardless of the number of people living in your home, I believe you can find opportunities for family prayer. In chapter one, we considered the benefits of praying for an unknown, future spouse. Recently, the Lord burdened my heart with a newfound appreciation for the power of prayers we can pray for the unknown, future child as well. In fact, during my wife's third pregnancy, I began to jot down a few prayers I was already lifting up for the baby we had yet to hold.

We prayed for our first two children, even while they were in the womb, but the Lord continues to stretch me in my prayer life for my family, which is exactly what he did during my prayers for baby #3. For those seeking to strengthen their family prayer times and for those who are praying for the Lord to bless them with a child or another child in the future, let me share some of the prayers I began to pray during my wife's pregnancy:

5 Things to Pray for the Unborn Child

1. **Pray that this baby would be fully dedicated to the Lord.** We will unpack this idea more in the next chapter, but to give you a preview, we look to 1 Samuel 1:11. Hannah prayed, even before she was pregnant, that the Lord would give her a child that would be fully dedicated to the Lord. He answered her prayer, and her son, Samuel, was given to God. Every child God gives will be devoted to something, passionate about something, investing their affections in something. Let it be the Lord, and let our prayers for such begin now.

2. **Praise the Lord for this blessing.** When Mary goes to visit Elizabeth in Luke 1, Elizabeth exclaimed, "Blessed is the fruit of your womb!" Now, the fruit of Mary's womb was Jesus, and the blessing He brought blessed all nations (Gen. 12:3; Gal. 3:8), but I still aim to emulate this outburst of praise that recognizes that the unborn child is, already, a blessing from the Lord. As James writes, every good gift is from above, coming down from the Father (James 1:17).

3. **Pray that this baby would walk well.** Every parent of a newborn longs for those first steps, that day that their baby pulls up and starts walking. We encourage these steps, we celebrate them, and we know they are part of healthy growth. In Colossians 1, Paul prays that the church would "walk in a manner worthy of the Lord." So before their first steps, before their first day, let us pray Colossians 1 over the baby in the womb, longing for the day they spiritually walk well, worthy of the Lord. And as they do, let us encourage these spiritual steps,

celebrate them, and recognize that they are part of healthy growth.

4. **Pray that this baby would know the Lord and His purpose.** The Bible speaks often about the unborn child. One of the most famous passages is Jeremiah's call in Jeremiah 1, when the Lord says to Jeremiah, "Before I formed you in the womb I knew you, and before you were born I consecrated you; I appointed you a prophet to the nations." Before he was born, Jeremiah was known by God, consecrated by God, and appointed by God. It is clear that the Lord has a plan and a purpose for the unborn child. And it's not just for Jeremiah. Psalm 139 proclaims that the Lord forms our inward parts and knits us together in our mother's womb, fearfully and wonderfully making us in his image, according to his purposes. He has ordained our days and so we pray that the next generation of babies will come to know God's sovereign will for their lives, and that they would obediently and passionately live out this calling. And we pray that they will not only know the Lord's will, but that they would also, simply put, know the Lord who formed them, for to know him is eternal life (John 17:3). Throughout each of our three pregnancies, my wife and I have prayed constantly that Gracie, Silas, and Elijah would come to know Jesus at an early age.

5. **Pray for purity.** Paul tells the young Timothy to set an example in speech, conduct, love, faith and purity (1 Timothy 4:12). As we live in a, seemingly, increasingly impure world, many of our prayers should focus on the last word of this verse, asking Christ for the purity of our children;

that they would, like young Timothy, set an example of purity to others; that they would, like Job, make a covenant with his eyes for the sake of purity (Job 31:1).

I know there are many more things we should pray for the unborn and born child, but here are five to get your family started as you continue to cultivate family prayer.

Family prayer has brought about some of my favorite moments. Family prayer affords me sweet insight into the hearts of my wife, daughter, and sons, insight that doesn't come any other way. We share our most profound desires, fears, needs, and praises when families pray together, and these prayers usually find families interceding for one another in powerful ways. This spiritual discipline, family intercession, is a biblical practice, modeled by men like Job, who would awake early in the morning in order to intercede on behalf of his seven sons and three daughters by offering a burnt sacrifice for their forgiveness.

We need Job-like families today who will get up early and intercede for their families in prayer.

We Intercede for our Families by Drawing Near to God

In Genesis 18, Abraham intercedes for his family, specifically, for his nephew, Lot. Now these two, Abraham and Lot, have a long history together. When God called Abraham to leave his home in Genesis 12, Abraham brought Lot with him. The two separate in chapter 13 because the land isn't big enough for both of them. At that point, Lot goes East to the Jordan Valley and settles in a city called Sodom. One chapter later, four kings invade the Jordan Valley, making war against five kings, including the King of Sodom. Lot is captured and taken away, and one man escapes the battle and runs to tell

Abram about the fate of his nephew, Lot. Abram immediately takes 318 trained men from his house and pursues the captors more than 120 miles on foot, defeating them in the night. He brings back all the possessions that had been stolen, as well as his nephew Lot. Then, we don't hear about Lot again until Genesis 18.

The Lord appears to Abraham and decides not to hide his will, but reveals what he's about to do. God is going to examine Sodom and Gomorrah to see if their actions are as bad as the outcry against them. Abraham immediately understands that this implies destruction. Destruction of Sodom and its people. Destruction of his relatives. Destruction of Lot.

Without delay, Abraham "draws near" to the Lord. This is the platform from which Abraham launches into intercession for his family.

We intercede for our families by first approaching God. Richard Foster writes, "One of the most critical aspects in learning to pray for others is to get in contact with God so that his life and power can flow through us into others. We begin praying for others by first quieting our fleshly activity and listening to the silent thunder of the Lord of hosts. Listening to the Lord is the first thing, the second thing, and the third thing necessary for successful intercession."[21]

Most of us have probably flown on an airplane before and, therefore, most of us are familiar with the flight attendant's instructions before takeoff. That's why we all ignore them. We're reading, texting, checking emails, and sleeping, all the while the flight attendants are attempting to educate us on the location of the exits, the appropriate way to fasten and unfasten our seatbelts, and the inevitability of the overhead luggage shifting during the flight. Finally, and perhaps most terrifying, they talk us through the oxygen masks. Modeling how to wear those yellow cups attached to plastic bags, they tell us that if we have kids sitting next to us, we are not to help them first. Challenging all of our parenting instincts, they instruct passengers to first put on their own oxygen masks before helping secure their child's oxygen mask.

This is how I understand the first part of family intercession. Before we can intercede for our family, we must breathe in Christ, draw near to Him, rest in Him, so that we may then lift up our spouse and children to the Lord. The power of our intercessory prayers comes from Christ, the one who intercedes for us. Hebrews 4:16 tells us that through Jesus Christ we are able to draw near to the throne of grace to find mercy, grace and help in our time of need. And I believe that as we draw near and are filled with the mercy, grace, and help of Christ, we are then prepared to pray for our families in their time of need.

We Intercede for our Families by Seeking the Character and Will of God

Richard Foster contends that "we must hear, know, and obey the will of God before we pray it into the lives of others."[22] In order to pray the will of God, we must be in a position to hear his will. His will then becomes the source of our bold, faithful prayers. As Scripture teaches, "This is the confidence that we have in him, that, if we ask any thing according to his will, he hears us" (1 John 5:14).

About 1,000 years ago, there was a monk and philosopher named Anselm who wrote a philosophical argument called "Proslogion," a "Discourse on the Existence of God." In this work, Anselm puts forth several deep theological questions that he then attempts to answer. He asks questions like, "How can God be perceived even though he isn't a body?" "How can God be just and show mercy to the wicked?" and "How can God justly punish and justly spare the wicked?"[23]

As Abraham seeks to know God's character and will before praying it for his family, he asks his own theological questions: "Will you sweep away the righteous with the wicked?" "Shall not the Judge of all the earth do what is just?" (Genesis 18:23-25)

Once these principles are established, Abraham discusses with God the fate of the righteous living in Sodom, presenting various hypothetical scenarios of the number of righteous living there. Each time, God's principle that he will not punish the righteous along with the wicked, is reaffirmed. They eventually go from discussing 50 people to 10, agreeing that if there are 10 righteous in the city, God will not destroy it. But he does destroy it in the next chapter and only three are rescued, illustrating the lack of 10 righteous in the city.

Your family may not live in Sodom, but they may be on a path toward destruction. They may not be in need of rescue from fire from heaven, but they do need deliverance from debt, sickness, sin, addiction, impurity, rebellion, depression, pornography, anxiety, hopelessness, doubt, apathy, selfishness, and unbelief. If we are to pray for our families, if we are to truly draw near to God and bring these urgent needs to Christ, we are to follow Abraham's example and begin by seeking to understand the character and will of the Lord. As E. Stanley Jones writes, "Prayer is surrender—surrender to the will of God and cooperation with that will. If I throw out a boathook from the boat and catch hold of the shore and pull, do I pull the shore to me, or do I pull myself to the shore? Prayer is not pulling God to my will, but the aligning of my will to the will of God."[24]

In the same way, The Westminster Catechism endorses the principle that, "Prayer is an offering up of our desires unto God, for things agreeable to His will."

Prayers that simply ask the Lord to bless all of our dreams and plans that we have established apart from God, are not the sort of powerful, intercessory prayers we see in Scripture. This isn't praying in the name of Jesus. This is praying in *our* name, according to *our* will. Instead of asking God to bless all of our wants, we are called to humbly seek his face, his heart, and his desires for our lives and families. When his will shapes our prayers and refines our requests, our intercession for our families will be molded to his will and we will find ourselves praying according to his name.

We Intercede for our Families by Lifting up the Broken

We've discussed how to pray for our families. The question now is, will we intercede? Will we pray? Do we care enough to fall to our knees? Does the brokenness around us move us to prayer? Is there a feeling of compassion and justice, a heart of love within us that will demand faithful, intercessory prayer?

Foster writes, "Frequently our lack is not faith but compassion. It seems that genuine empathy between the (one praying) and the (one prayed for) often makes the difference. Jesus was 'moved with compassion' for people...If we have God-given compassion and concern for others, our faith will grow and strengthen as we pray. In fact, if we genuinely love people, we desire for them far more than it is within our power to give, and that will cause us to pray."[25]

Families are broken, and this should move us. We should be filled with compassion, desiring more than we can give, leaving us in a spirit of dependence with a heart to pray. This is one of the most significant things we could ever do for our families. What a privilege to have the invitation to enter into the presence of Jesus and be heard! It is far too easy to see the unhealthy aspects of our homes and do nothing. It is far too easy to hope for nothing and pray for nothing.

My prayer is that we will become families of prayer. Just as Jesus had a zeal that his house would be a house of prayer (Matthew 21:13), I pray that we too would pursue, with great passion, a house of prayer. A house where we draw near to God. A house where we pray the Lord's will for our families. A house where we respond to the broken and unhealthy with bold, tireless intercession.

One practical way we can begin to create a house of prayer is by using a family prayer journal. When we record prayer requests from one another, journal our prayers for our families, and write down all of the praises and answered prayers we see in our home, I believe we will find everyone in the house enjoying prayer and looking forward to praying together.

Praying Scripture over our families is another practical example of integrating prayer into the home.

Praying Scripture over our Families

Just about every book of the Bible contains a prayer that carries timeless truths and promises related to God's character and heart for his people. Years ago, I began praying a prayer from the book of Colossians for my wife. Once we welcomed our first child into the home, I started praying this prayer for both my wife and daughter, and years later, I now pray this prayer for my wife and all three of our children:

> "We have not ceased to pray for you, asking that you may be filled with the knowledge of his will in all spiritual wisdom and understanding, so as to walk in a manner worthy of the Lord, fully pleasing to him, bearing fruit in every good work and increasing in the knowledge of God. May you be strengthened with all power, according to his glorious might, for all endurance and patience with joy, giving thanks to the Father, who has qualified you to share in the inheritance of the saints in light" (Colossians 1:9-12).

I began to discover other prayers in the Bible that I wanted prayed over our home. I shared this with some other families and found that many of my friends were also praying Scripture over their families. Our Gospel Family Ministry put together a collection of 31 of these biblical passages and gave the family devotion, *31 Days of Praying Scripture Over Your Family*, away for free on iBooks and our website (gospelfamily.org). Perhaps this challenge, one month of praying one Scripture a day for your family, is the best way for you to introduce a renewed sense of prayer to your home.

Allow me to share these passages and some examples of prayers with you here:

A Prayer for Blessing: "The Lord bless you and keep you; the Lord make his face to shine upon you and be gracious to you; the Lord lift up his countenance upon you and give you peace" (Numbers 6:24-26).

Father, we pray that you will bless our family. We don't ask for worldly blessings, but for the good gifts of grace that can only come from you. We are in desperate need of you and we don't want to live one day separated from your perfect love. Bless us with your presence. Bless us with your sanctification. Bless us with unity, faithfulness, and the opportunity to passionately live your mission. Thank you for your limitless grace that is daily upon us. We praise you for allowing your face to shine on our family and for filling us with a peace that this world cannot understand.

A Prayer for Unity: "I do not ask for these only, but also for those who will believe in me through their word, that they may all be one, just as you, Father are in me, and I in you, that they also may be in us, so that the world may believe that you have sent me" (John 17:20-21).

Jesus, thank you for your prayers for us. You are indeed our Intercessor and we praise you this morning. We echo your prayer and ask that you will draw us to yourself, allowing us to be one with you. Unify us together by teaching us to align our desires, goals, hopes, and prayers with your will. I pray that our family will be a unified family without discord. Thank you for the unity with which you have already blessed us. Let us agree in Spirit and in prayer so that those who know our family may honor your name.

A Prayer for Salvation: "Brothers, my heart's desire and prayer to God for them is that they may be saved" (Romans 10:1).

We pray, this morning, for salvation. We eagerly wait for a future day of salvation when our children will come to know you as their Savior, Lord, Forgiver, Redeemer, Healer, Hope, True Love, Protector, and as their very Life. I pray that you will continue to pursue them as a fierce Warrior and passionate Lover. Draw us to your side. We pray that our children will come to know you at a young age and that they will follow after you with all of their affections for all of their days. I ask that you give us, as parents, the wisdom and grace to disciple our children and encourage them in the faith. We trust them in your hands, Father, knowing that you sent your Son to seek and to save.

A Prayer of Thanksgiving: "We always thank God, the Father of our Lord Jesus Christ, when we pray for you, since we heard of your faith in Christ Jesus and of the love that you have for all the saints, because of the hope laid up for you in heaven" (Colossians 1:3-5).

Our heart is filled with thanksgiving. Our lives are filled with blessings. For years now, you Lord have allowed us to live this blessed life with our wonderful family. I offer up a prayer of thanksgiving this morning for my beautiful bride. Thank you for graciously bringing her into my life. I can't imagine a day without her. I praise you for her example of faith in you—the way she trusts you with her life, our family, our future, and everything in between. I praise you for her love that springs forth into my heart, truly reflecting your love for us all.

A Prayer for Maturity: "We have not ceased to pray for you, asking that you may be filled with the knowledge of his will in all spiritual wisdom and understanding, so as to walk in a manner worthy of the Lord, fully pleasing to him, bearing fruit in every good work and increasing in the knowledge of God. May you be strengthened with all power, according to his glorious might, for all endurance and patience with joy, giving thanks to the Father, who has qualified you to share in the inheritance of the saints in light" (Colossians 1:9-12).

We seek you, Father. We seek your counsel, your word, your guidance. Fill us with the knowledge of your will for our family. How should we love one another? How should we disciple our children? What ministry should consume us? How are we to use our gifts and creativity for your glory? What open door is there for missions? Where are you leading? How can we follow? We need you, Father. Reveal your will for us so that we may live worthy of you and your calling; so that we may please and honor you; so that we may bear fruit and grow in our spiritual maturity. Strengthen us this morning with your power so that we may patiently endure as we wait

93

for you to lead us in the next step. As always, we trust in you.

A Prayer for the Fruit of Righteousness: "And it is my prayer that your love may abound more and more, with knowledge and all discernment, so that you may approve what is excellent, and so be pure and blameless for the day of Christ, filled with the fruit of righteousness that comes through Jesus Christ, to the glory and praise of God" (Philippians 1:9-11).

We know love because of you, Jesus. I pray that our family will exhibit your love and that our understanding of and delight in your love for us will abound more and more. Lord, give us the gift of discernment so that we may know how our family can best honor you. I pray that you will keep us pure and blameless, living lives above reproach so that we may be presented to you as your Bride upon your glorious return. Come quickly Lord Jesus! Fill us with the fruit of righteousness that can only come from you. Let us be a light to the world that points them to you to the glory and praise of your holy name!

A Prayer of Exaltation: "I will extol you, my God and King, and bless your name forever and ever. Every day I will bless you and praise your name forever and ever. Great is the Lord, and greatly to be praised, and his greatness is unsearchable" (Psalm 145:1-3).

You are worthy of praise. You are worthy of worship. You deserve our undivided affection, our unwavering devotion. To honor and glorify you is to simply ascribe to you what is already due your name. To fail to exalt you is to rob you of what is rightfully yours. We do exalt your name today, Jesus. You are our King and for all of our lives, we will praise you. We will sing your name, pray your name, glorify your name, and proclaim your name: Jesus! You are holy and altogether different than anything this world has to offer. You are perfectly and limitlessly powerful. You have proven yourself, over and over again, to be beautifully good to our family. The Psalmist was right: Your greatness, no one can fathom.

A Prayer of Rejoicing: "My heart exults in the Lord; my horn is exalted in the Lord. My mouth derides my enemies, because I rejoice in your salvation. There is none holy like the Lord: for there is none besides you; there is no rock like our God" (1 Samuel 2:1-2).

Our heart rejoices in you, Lord. You said you came to give us an abundant life and to make our joy complete and you have been perfectly faithful in your promise. Life with our family, friends, and church is an abundant, joyful life. So, this morning, we rejoice. We offer up a prayer of rejoicing to you God. We praise you for your deliverance from our slavery to sin, the strongholds of sin, and the cares of this world. No one else could give us the life that you've given. No one else could deliver us as you have. There is, indeed, no one else like you. Thank you, Jesus for giving us so many reasons to be joyful, so many reasons to praise you, so many reasons to simply rejoice!

A Prayer for Forgiveness: "When heaven is shut up and there is no rain because they have sinned against you, if they pray toward this place and acknowledge your name and turn from their sin, when you afflict them, then hear in heaven and forgive the sin of your servants, your people Israel, when you teach them the good way in which they should walk, and grant rain upon your land, which you have given to your people as an inheritance. Now, O my God, let your eyes be open and your ears attentive to the prayer of this place" (2 Chronicles 6:26-27, 40).

Hear our prayers, our God. Forgive us of our sins. We confess to you that we have fallen short of your calling. I do not live as the one you created me to be. I agree with you that I am not fit to be in your righteous presence, Father. Cleanse me of all unrighteousness and cover me with the atoning, purifying blood of your Son. I pray that you will no longer remember my sin or see my sin when you look at me. Instead, I ask that, by your grace and mercy, you will see the righteousness of Christ. Give me the strength, discipline, desire, and grace I need to turn from sin, repent of my sinful habits, flee from the temptations of the world, and live like you; and live for you. Thank you for covering our family with grace!

A Prayer for Intimacy: "How lovely is your dwelling place, O Lord of hosts! My soul longs, yes, faints for the courts of the Lord; my heart and flesh sing for joy to the living God" (Psalm 84:1-2).

There is nothing greater than delighting in your presence. There is nothing sweeter than simply knowing you. How privileged we are to be able to call you, Father! We are hungry for more of you, Lord. Our soul cries out for you even when our flesh pulls away. We ask that you will give our family deeper, more intimate relationships with you. Show us how to truly seek you in the mornings and chase after you all day long. We pray that our time in your Word and in your presence will be life transforming for us and glorifying to you. Increase our desire for you to the point that we are fainting for you. Through your Holy Spirit, Jesus, usher us into your presence this morning and let us intimately rest there throughout the day.

A Prayer for Sanctification: "Sanctify them in the truth; your word is truth. As you sent me into the world, so I have sent them into the world. And for their sake I consecrate myself, that they also may be sanctified in truth" (John 17:17-19).

Set us apart, Jesus. Let our family be different. I pray that I will truly love my spouse as you love the church. I pray that you will always be the love of my spouse's life and that we will reflect you to the nations. We pray that our children will truly find their identity in you, Jesus, and never be of the world. Let us be light in the darkness. Let us be a stark contrast as we live as aliens here. This is not our home! Let us be holy as you are holy. Pour your word over us today and sanctify us by the powerful, effective, living, active truth of your word.

A Prayer for Strength: "Uphold me according to your promise, that I may live, and let me not be put to shame in my hope!" (Psalm 119:116)

We lay our hopes at your feet. Our dreams for tomorrow, our goals for the future, our desires for our family...we lay all of this at your feet, Lord. We pray for strength this morning. We ask that you strengthen us when we're weak, exhausted, discouraged, defeated. Strengthen us so that we may fulfill your calling for our family's dreams, hopes, desires and goals. We want these to honor you, but it is often difficult to keep our eyes fixed on you, the

Author of our faith, salvation and lives. Strengthen us with endurance to run and finish the race with our eyes fixed on no one but you.

A Prayer for Provision: "Our Father in heaven, hallowed be your name. Your kingdom come, your will be done, on earth as it is in heaven. Give us this day our daily bread, and forgive us our debts, as we also have forgiven our debtors. And lead us not into temptation, but deliver us from evil" (Matthew 6:9-13).

Father, holy is your name. We pray for your will to be done in our family. Thank you for providing for us everyday. We ask that you continue to provide what we need, physically, financially, and spiritually. In everything, we need you. In everything, we depend on you. Keep us from chasing things we don't need. Instead, teach us the disciplines of simplicity and contentment. We praise you for all you have given us. You are indeed our Provider.

A Prayer of Dedication: "O Lord of hosts, if you will indeed look on the affliction of your servant and remember me and not forget your servant, but will give to your servant a son, then I will give him to the Lord all the days of his life, and no razor shall touch his head. For this child I prayed, and the Lord has granted me my petition that I made to him. Therefore I have lent him to the Lord. As long as he lives, he is lent to the Lord" (1 Samuel 1:10-11; 27-28).

Our children, O Lord, are among the most amazing blessings in the world and we worship you for these adorable gifts. We love them with everything we have, and yet, we know that you love them even more. You knew them before the foundation of the world and they belong to you. Thank you for answering years of prayers and blessing us with such a wonderful family. We now give this family back to you. We dedicate our children to you, your will, your service, your calling, and your glory. Use them to further your kingdom and exalt your name. Nothing would bring us greater joy as parents. For their whole life, they will be given over to you Lord.

A Prayer for Completion: "I thank my God in all my remembrance of you, always in every prayer of mine for you all making my prayer with joy, because of your partnership in the gospel from the first day until now. And I am sure of this, that he who began a good work in you will bring it to completion at the day of Jesus Christ" (Philippians 1:3-6).

You have been working in our lives individually and as a family now for years Lord. You have redeemed us, molded us, matured us, and used us as your messengers and servants. You saved us from our sin and made us new creations. We pray that you will help us endure the rest of the race. We trust you to complete all that you have begun in us. Don't give up on us. Don't stop working in us, sanctifying us to look more like you. Continue to send us out as your messengers. We ask that you forcefully carry out your good work in our lives until it is complete on the day of your glorious return.

A Prayer for Protection: "I have given them your word, and the world has hated them because they are not of the world, just as I am not of the world. I do not ask that you take them out of the world, but that you keep them from the evil one. They are not of the world, just as I am not of the world." (John 17:14-16).

With all of the potential dangers and threats present in the world, we realize, Father, that our greatest battle is not against flesh and blood. We know that we have an enemy seeking to devour us and lead us away from you. We also know that we have a Defender, a Warrior Protector. We pray that you will protect us from the god of this age. Protect us from the evil one of the world as we live as lights in this world. Let us be in the world but not of it. Protect our family from the lies of the accuser. Protect our family from the attacks of the devil. Protect us, Lord, from the temptations of our enemy. Let us put on the armor of God each morning as we fight the good fight of faith.

A Prayer for Mercy: "Have mercy on me, O God, according to your steadfast love; according to your abundant mercy blot out my transgressions. Wash me thoroughly from my iniquity, and cleanse me from my sin!" (Psalm 51:1-2).

You know we have sinned, Lord. We confess to you that we have disobeyed your commandments and have quenched your Holy Spirit while yielding to our flesh. Have mercy on our family. Jesus, pour down the forgiveness that we do not deserve. Let us be covered in your unfailing love. Please do not remember us according to our failures and transgressions. Remove sin from us as far as the east is from the west. Wash us clean, Jesus. Purify our hearts and minds so that we may stand in your holy presence, unblemished. Thank you Jesus for dying on the cross for our sins. We give you worship this morning for your mercy.

A Prayer of Adoration: "You have led in your steadfast love the people whom you have redeemed; you have guided them by your strength to your holy abode. The Lord will reign forever and ever" (Exodus 15:13, 18).

Lord, we come to you this morning to simply adore you. Your love is breathtaking. Your leadership of our family is indispensable. Your redemption, immeasurable. Your strength, powerful. Your guidance, essential. Your holiness, incomparable. There is no one like you. Only you are Lord and our family will serve no other one. Our family will worship no one else. Our family will honor no other king. Our family will adore no other god. For there is no one worthy of our adoration but you. You reign from generation to generation. You reign from eternity past to eternity future. Your kingdom has no end. We are in awe of you for you are awesome. To just know you, God, is life itself. Thank you for revealing yourself to us.

A Prayer for Help: "I called out to the Lord, out of my distress, and he answered me; out of the belly of Sheol I cried, and you heard my voice" (Jonah 2:2).

We take great comfort in the truth that you, Jesus, went through all of the struggles and trials of life and can now sympathize with us in our weaknesses. You are our High Priest who knows what difficulties this life can bring. We come to you with our needs, our hurts, and our battles. Help us. We cry out for your help, knowing that we need you; knowing that we can't make it alone; knowing that you love us and know what we need before we even ask for it. Listen to our plea this morning. Give attention to our hearts and prayers. Answer us as we wait for you in the depths of the sea. Help us Lord. Bring us the healing, provision, and deliverance for which we are desperate today.

A Prayer for Justice: "O Lord, God of Abraham, Isaac, and Israel, let it be known this day that you are God in Israel, and that I am your servant, and that I have done all these things at your word. Answer me, O Lord, answer me, that this people may know that you, O Lord, are God, and that you have turned their hearts back" (1 Kings 18:36-37).

We long for the world to know you Lord. We long to see the unrighteous fall to their knees and acknowledge that you are the Savior of the world. Turn their hearts to you. We trust you with the judgment of all peoples and are drowning in your grace that allows us, redeemed sinners, to be in right standing with you. Use us to make you known among the nations. Send us to the dark corners of the world that currently rob you of the glory you deserve. Let it be known among all peoples that you Jesus are Lord, and we are your humble servants. In the midst of so much injustice in the world—poverty, abuse, neglect, trafficking, genocide, and the perversion of truth—prove yourself just.

A Prayer for our Enemies: And as they were stoning Stephen, he called out, "Lord Jesus, receive my spirit." And falling to his knees he cried out with a loud voice, "Lord, do not hold this sin against them" (Acts 7:59-60).

Jesus, you commanded us to pray for our enemies. Thank you for modeling this for us and for giving us examples through other faithful believers. We do pray for those who have hurt us. There have been those who have personally attacked us, who have gossiped about us behind our backs, and who have maliciously resisted our attempts at friendship. Forgive them of their sins. Lead them to you and take away their evil desires. We ask that you will free us from any bitterness or resentment, and reveal to us our own sin against that person so that we might confess and seek restoration in the relationship. Do not hold their sin against them, but instead, use us to model your grace and forgiveness. Use us to demonstrate your love.

A Prayer for God's Will: And going a little farther, he fell on the ground and prayed that, if it were possible, the hour might pass from him. And he said, "Abba, Father, all things are possible for you. Remove this cup from me. Yet not what I will, but what you will" (Mark 14:35-36).

How often does our will get in your way? How often do we lead ourselves rather than following you? Discipline us today, Lord. Teach us how to truly live as Christ Followers. Take away our will and give us the desires of your heart. You are the Potter. We are the clay. Mold us according to your good and perfect purpose for our lives. We know that you love us. We know that you created us with a purpose. We know that everything you do is for your glory. So we follow fearlessly, completely trusting in you, Lord.

A Prayer for Missionaries: "Praying at all times in the Spirit, with all prayer and supplication. To that end keep alert with all perseverance, making supplication for all the saints, and also for me, that words may be given to me in opening my mouth boldly to proclaim the mystery of the gospel, for which I am an ambassador in chains, that I may declare it boldly, as I ought to speak" (Ephesians 6:18-20).

Oh let the nations be glad and rejoice over the great salvation of the Christ! We ask for you, the Lord of the harvest, to send out more laborers into your mission fields. We praise you for our partners in the Gospel, our friends and fellow believers who have left homes and families in order to take your gospel to the lost. Bless their ministries. Speak through them so that they may fearlessly proclaim the Gospel of grace. We pray for our missionary friends this morning serving across the street and across the world. We lift up the teams of missionaries laboring among the unreached, proclaiming the Gospel to those who have yet to hear. We pray that the words they speak will be your words and that your words will serve as healing for the nations.

A Prayer of Supplication: "Do not be anxious about anything, but in everything by prayer and supplication with thanksgiving let your requests be made known to God" (Philippians 4:6).

We bring our needs to you today. With thanksgiving for all you have already given, for all of the prayers you have already answered, we present our requests to you Father. We pray for a blessed, protected marriage. Let us intimately and passionately live a life that seeks holiness. Equip us to know how to be the parents that our children need so that they will know your love and our love for them. We lift up our families to you this morning. We ask that you will draw them to you and reveal to them your involvement in their lives. We also intercede for our church and our friends. We pray for unity for the church and spiritual maturity for our friends.

A Prayer for Wisdom: "And now, O Lord my God, you have made your servant king in place of David my father, although I am but a little child. I do not know how to go out or come in. And your servant is in the midst of your people whom you have chosen, a great people, too many to be numbered or counted for multitude. Give your servant therefore an understanding mind to govern your people, that I may discern between good and evil, for who is able to govern this your great people?" (1 Kings 3:7-9)

Help us not to be a family that lacks godly wisdom. Let us never settle for worldly wisdom, but let us seek after your voice through your word and prayer so that we may receive the gift of discernment. Allow us to know what is right and wrong, even in the most difficult situations. As we make decisions, we ask that we will be unified in Spirit and that our decisions will be founded upon godly wisdom. We pray this morning for wisdom. We pray for wisdom from above that is "pure, peaceable, gentle, open to reason, full of mercy and good fruits, impartial, and sincere" (James 3:17). We trust that you, God, give generously to all without finding fault.

A Prayer for Boldness: "And now, Lord, look upon their threats and grant to your servants to continue to speak your word with all boldness, while you stretch out your hand to heal, and signs and wonders are performed through the name of your holy servant Jesus" (Acts 4:29-30).

Jesus, we do not want to live safe, boring lives. We do not want to shy away from living your mission. We do not want to run from worthy challenges in order to pursue comfort. Protect us from the soft life. Give us boldness to speak your name and live your adventure. Let us live on the edge of all that you are doing. Let us long for the unexpected, pray for holy moments of spontaneity, and rejoice when unforeseen surprises radically transform our lives. Fill us with your bold Spirit, and shake our world!

A Prayer of Praise for Redemption: "Blessed be the Lord God of Israel, for he has visited and redeemed his people" (Luke 1:68).

Jesus, we praise you for freedom! We praise you for redemption! Had you not come to rescue us, while we were still dead in our sins, we would still be slaves to our sins. But you have purchased us by your blood. We have been bought with a price and we are not our own. Let us not live for ourselves and return to our old life of slavery. But let us live for you, our Master who bought us. You have ushered in a spiritual year of jubilee and our chains are gone. You have rescued us from our flesh, this world, and the evil one. Only you, Jesus, could create in us a clean heart and transform us into new creations. Our family worships you this morning for the redemption that fills our hearts and souls.

A Prayer for the Nations: "Lord, now you are letting your servant depart in peace, according to your word; for my eyes have seen your salvation that you have prepared in the presence of all peoples, a light for revelation to the Gentiles, and for glory to your people Israel" (Luke 2:29-32).

Father, let us be found faithful to pray for the nations. Let us be found faithful to intercede on behalf of the tribes, tongues and peoples of your world. They are created in your image for your glory and we pray for their salvation. Send missionaries to every people group so that they may hear of your grace and truth and come to know you as their Savior. We pray that you meet their physical needs in the midst of unbelievable suffering. We ask that you meet their spiritual needs in the midst of unimaginable darkness. Reveal your love for the nations to the nations.

A Prayer for God's Glory: "Not to us, O Lord, not to us, but to your name give glory, for the sake of your steadfast love and your faithfulness!" (Psalm 115:1)

Exalt your name, Jesus! Make known your fame and power among the nations. Let all people come and bow down and worship you. May all families of all tribes and tongues sing songs of praise to your glorious name. We pray that you will receive the glory that is rightfully yours. We pray that we will glorify you today. Let us never rob you of worship. May we daily turn all praise back to you. You have blessed us so that we might bless you and lead others to do the same. We pray for opportunities, even today, to bring you glory. I pray that the way that our family loves one another will be honoring to you. We glorify your name this morning, Jesus.

A Prayer for the Church: "And let the peace of Christ rule in your hearts, to which indeed you were called in one body. And be thankful. Let the word of Christ dwell in you richly, teaching and admonishing one another in all wisdom, singing psalms and hymns and spiritual songs, with thankfulness in your hearts to God. And whatever you do, in word or deed, do everything in the name of the Lord Jesus, giving thanks to God the Father through him" (Colossians 3:15-17).

Lord Jesus, we have fallen in love with your Bride. We long to present her to you, pure and blameless, upon your return. We pray for the church this morning. We pray that your peace will reign in their hearts so that she might be unified as one Body. Let your gracious, freeing, living message be in the center of their hearts and on the tip of their tongues. We ask that they will teach, admonish, encourage, challenge, serve, and love one another every day of the week. Let our words and actions serve as faithful testimonies to the rest of the world. Let us boldly be the church for your glory!

A Prayer of Thanksgiving for our Family: "Oh give thanks to the Lord; call upon his name; make known his deeds among the peoples! Sing to him, sing praises to him; tell of all his wondrous works!" (Psalm 105:1-2)

We will never be able to give you enough thanks, Lord, for the gift of this family. Thank you for being the Author of our story and for being sovereign as you brought us together under your will and for your glory. We call on your name this morning Jesus to sing a prayer of praise to you for all of your provision and gifts of grace. We cannot say enough. We will never stop telling of your blessings over our family. Let us shout from the rooftops that you are good, giving, gracious, and the source of everything beautiful. Thank you for our family!

Family Discussion Questions

1. How often does your family pray together?

2. How often do you pray for your family?

3. What prayer needs does your family have today?

4. What time of the day could you devote to family prayer?

5. Why do you believe it's important to strengthen this spiritual discipline in your home?

6. What prayers have you seen the Lord answer already in your family?

7. Why is it important to pray God's will for our families, and what would need to change for this to take place more often in your home?

CHAPTER 8

Gospel Parenting

How to make Jesus Indignant

MY WIFE LOVES GARAGE SALES. So when she called me one Saturday and said that she and the kids would be down the street at our neighbor's garage sale, it didn't surprise me at all. By the time I made it home, the garage sale was over, but my family was still there. My kids were in the front yard playing with my neighbors' kids, while my wife was talking with the children's mother.

We spent the afternoon in their living room, getting to know each other while our kids ran around the house and up and down the street. The wife of the family told us that her mom was disappointed that she didn't have very many kids. This surprised me because she had six kids, twice as many as we have. Apparently, in her culture in Southern Sudan, families typically have many more children.

She told me, 15 children is not uncommon. Children fill the house, and they see this as a blessing.

What a refreshing worldview of children! Not a hassle.

Not an inconvenience. Not noisy or expensive or annoying or messy, but a gift from God. I say this is refreshing because it's biblical.

"Children are a heritage from the Lord, the fruit of the womb a reward...Blessed is the man who fills his quiver with them." (Psalm 127:3)

Children are from God and should be dedicated to God (1 Samuel 1:27-28) and led to Christ.

In the Gospels, many families longed to see their children at the feet of the Savior. They pressed through the crowds, bringing their children to Jesus, like the men who dug a hole in the roof so that their paralyzed friend could see the Lord.

The disciples tried to stop this. Maybe they didn't have a biblical worldview of children. Maybe they saw them as an inconvenience or unimportant or as a distraction.

And this—this hindrance, this attitude—made Jesus indignant.

Jesus said, "Let the children come to me; do not hinder them, for to such belongs the kingdom of God." (Mark 10:14)

I believe one of the surest ways to make Jesus indignant is to keep children from the Lord, and I believe one of the surest ways to keep our children from the Lord is to fail to view them as a heritage from the Lord.

Kids are gifts. Gifts that should be given right back to the Giver. And the Gospel truth is that when we lead our children to Jesus, they become children all over again, adopted as sons and daughters into the Family of God.

Dedicated to the Lord

Have you ever wanted something so badly that you couldn't even eat? Have you ever prayed for something so fervently that others thought you were intoxicated? When was the last time you wept bitterly as you prayed? Such were the prayers of Hannah, a childless wife in 1 Samuel.

She pleads with the Lord for a child, asking God to give her a son. Her desperate longing is unmistakable; her desire, heartfelt. What's surprising, however, about her prayers, is the vow she makes to the Lord. Hannah prays, "O Lord of hosts, if you will indeed look on the affliction of your servant and remember me and not forget your servant, but will give to your servant a son, then I will give him to the Lord all the days of his life" (1 Samuel 1:11).

Here's a woman surrounded by children, but with no children of her own. Here's a woman asking God for a son while simultaneously promising to give any future son right back to the Lord.

Can we imagine making such a vow? Can we imagine a heart that is prepared to surrender everything to God? Can we relate to someone who is willing to submit to the Lord that which is nearest and dearest? How many parents have we met who joyfully devote their children to the will of the Lord?

Soon after praying her desperate prayer, Hannah gives birth to a baby boy named Samuel, and she proves faithful to fulfill her vow. After nursing the baby for some time, Hannah takes Samuel to the house of the Lord and dedicates him for as long as he will live.

It seems so simple, dedicating our children to the Lord. We have a "baby dedication service" twice a year at the church I pastor, one at Christmas and another on Mother's Day. Lately, these services have been pretty full, as our families have welcomed 12-15 new babies a year for several years running. I love these special services. It's beautiful to see parents standing at the front of the sanctuary, holding their newborn babies, committing to the church that they aim to disciple their children in the way of the Lord, while asking the church to partner with them in this ministry.

We present each family with a new Bible that can be read to their children and, one day, read by their children. Other families stand with them as we pray, asking Jesus to grant us all the wisdom and grace needed to devote these precious gifts to the one who gave them in the first place.

Once the service is over, I always wonder what challenges these families will face as they strive to live out their vow of dedication. What will threaten their desire to surrender their family to Christ? Will the test come when their son asks if he can play baseball instead of gathering with the church? Or when Family Worship conflicts with Monday Night Football? Will it be when their daughter feels called to move overseas as a missionary to a dangerous people?

Will these families be called to follow the example of Zebedee who stood silently in the boat as his two sons, James and John, stepped out, left everything, and followed Jesus? I just picture this man standing there, watching his sons, the ones who were to take care of him as he ages—provide for him, run the family business, and serve as his retirement plan—stepping out, leaving everything behind in order to follow the Christ. It reminds me of my parents dropping me off at the airport when I was 23, willingly sending me to live in the depths of the Peruvian jungles for the next two years. It reminds me of all of the faithful parents who have dedicated their children to the Lord by supporting their dedication to the Lord, valuing obedience over safety.

A call to dedicate our children is a call to embrace the words of A.W. Tozer, realizing that "everything is safe which we commit to him, and nothing is really safe which is not so committed"?[26]

Dedicating our children to the Lord is a call to seek the Lord's will for their lives, no matter how unpopular, how inconvenient, how uncomfortable, or how dangerous. It is a call to submit our dreams for them to the plan Jesus has for them. A call to recognize that, long before we named them, Christ knew them. Long before we loved them, Jesus died for them, and they, therefore, belong to him.

Parenting is stewardship; taking care of that which belongs

to Jesus in such a way that pleases Jesus, glorifies Jesus, and points our children to Jesus.

Leading Messy Kids to Jesus

My wife went to the store one night, leaving me with all three kids.

It was just an hour or so, and the night started off calm. My 4-year-old and 2-year-old were coloring together at the kitchen table while my newborn baby was sleeping in the next room. A few minutes later, the baby woke up and so I went to the other room to be with him. I was gone for about 15 minutes, apparently the exact amount of time needed for a disaster.

I returned to the kitchen.

Good news, my kids were still coloring. Bad news, they were completely naked and were coloring themselves.

They were covered from head to toe, with Braveheart-like face paint. They had even colored the entire kitchen table, covering it with a dark red outlined in pink. They had shaded in the blue high chair with a bright orange and left little green fingerprints on everything they had touched.

I started the bathtub. And then my wife returned from the store.

Two days later, my kids were with me in my office. As I met with someone in one room, they went into the closest bathroom and turned on the water, somehow clogging the drain in the process. Minutes later, the sink overflowed onto them and the floor, creating their ideal splash pad, which they enjoyed loudly.

When I opened the door, waves carried them out of the bathroom into my office.

Needless to say, I've been reminded often that kids are messy. They're dirty, muddy, wet, slimy, and inexplicably so. But it's not just their faces, noses, feet and hands. Their hearts are dirty, too; or, better put, their hearts are desperately sick. So what do we do with these messy kids?

A bath will wash away the Crayola and finger paint. Washing machines may take care of grass stains, and a tissue will clear that nose right up. But the heart needs more than a wet wipe and hand sanitizer.

All kids are messy and all messy kids need Christ.

I love the way Paul describes this need and how it's met:

"At one time we too were foolish, disobedient, deceived and enslaved by all kinds of passions and pleasures. We lived in malice and envy, being hated and hating one another" (Titus 3:3).

That's pretty messy.

"But when the kindness and love of God our Savior appeared, he saved us, not because of righteous things we had done, but because of his mercy. He saved us through the washing of rebirth and renewal by the Holy Spirit, whom he poured out on us generously through Jesus Christ our Savior, so that, having been justified by his grace, we might become heirs having the hope of eternal life" (Titus 3:4-7).

We react quickly and decisively when we see our kids covered in dirt. We pick them up and bring them to the bath. Let the Gospel Family be as intentional when we see the sinful condition of our kids. Let us graciously and lovingly pick them up and bring them to Christ for the washing of rebirth and renewal by the Spirit.

Parenting with Grace

Dedicating our children to the Lord is sort of a big picture idea. It's looking at the breadth of parenting and resolving to submit it all to Christ. Within this grand vision, however, are individual years, months, weeks, and days. Parenting is a series of moments—messy and otherwise—strung together. And each one of these moments need to be seasoned with grace.

Grace in the home will create an atmosphere of love and forgiveness, inviting a spirit of humility and freedom. Instead of exhausting ourselves trying to shape the outward behavior of our children by enforcing a list of house rules, let us exhaust ourselves in our prayers, asking Christ to transform their hearts. Behavior modification will never save our children and since their salvation, their discipleship, their sanctification, are to rest as our greatest desire, their hearts must be our greatest prayer.

Pastor Mason shares, "Many times when I am discipling my sons, I become so agitated by their actions that I forget the gospel. I forget mercy, love, grace, and, most of all, I forget I am supposed to be helping them to understand forgiveness. Without the gospel, I am only projecting behavioral modification. Change of heart must trump mere change of behavior."[27]

Timothy Keller writes about this contrast between an outward and an inward change. "Self-salvation through good works may produce a great deal of moral behavior in your life, but inside you are filled with self-righteousness, cruelty, and bigotry, and you are miserable," Keller writes. "You cannot, therefore, deal with your hideousness and self-absorption through the moral law, by trying to be a good person through an act of the will. You need a complete transformation of the very motives of your heart."[28]

Keller goes on to say that the devil may actually even prefer that we turn into Pharisees who are attempting to save themselves.[29] When we welcome grace into our home, it frees us from the shackles of parenting by law, of earning love and favor, and blesses us with the joy of relying on Jesus to move within our hearts.

I remember trying to teach and model grace to my daughter when she was two years old. We were in the car, driving home, and dessert was waiting at the house. Cake, I think. My daughter, Gracie, had been waiting for this dessert, looking forward to it and talking about it all night long. Nothing would come between Gracie and her piece of cake once she burst through the front door. Unfortunately, something came between them long before we pulled into the driveway.

She had refused to leave the home we were at earlier that evening. Like most kids, she wanted to stay and play with her friends and couldn't understand why that couldn't last well into the middle of the night. By the time we got her buckled into her car seat, my wife and I were frustrated and Gracie was bawling. At some point, I had said, "Gracie, if you don't come right now, you will not get any of your cake when we get home." She did not come at that point either, securing for herself a cake-less night.

It was pretty quiet as we drove home.

Now, usually, I stick to these sort of punishments. I keep my word. If I tell her I'm going to put her in time-out, take her stuffed animals out of her bed, or take away a toy, I follow through. On this particular night, though, I decided to use it as an opportunity to teach my daughter about grace.

Back home, I sat down with Gracie, tears still running down her cheeks, and I tried to talk about the grace of Christ to a two year old. It went something like this:

Me: *"Do you know why we named you, 'Gracie'"?*

Gracie: *"Why?"*

Me: *"Because Jesus shows us grace and we wanted that to be your name. Do you know what 'grace' is?"*

Gracie: *"No."*

Me: *"Grace is a blessing or a gift that God gives us even though we don't deserve it. When Jesus died on the cross for our sins, he gave us the greatest gift, but we didn't deserve this gift."*

Gracie: *"We don't deserve it because we sin?"*

Me: *"That's right. But Jesus gives us this gift anyway. That's an example of grace. So tonight, I want to show you grace and give you what you don't deserve."*

I gave her a piece of cake that night, and we actually spent the rest of the evening in this wonderful conversation about grace and the cross and Jesus and forgiveness. It was beautiful. I was so proud of our little theological and grace-based parenting moment. Of course, the next day, Gracie turned the tables on me. We were in the car again, heading home for Gracie's nap when she called out from the back seat.

"Daddy," she said. "Do you remember that word you taught me last night? You know, that word about Jesus dying on the cross for us and how we don't deserve it because of our sin."

"Do you mean, 'grace?'" I asked.

"Yes," she answered. "So, can you show me grace and let me skip my nap today?"

Twenty-four hours of enjoying the grace of the cross and she was already using it to get out of a nap. I didn't fall for it, though. She took a long nap that day.

Years later, my wife and I are continuingly seeking ways to show grace to our kids. We try to find those little moments, small opportunities, to speak words of grace and give examples of the same. I fail at this more than not, but I press on, for I have become convinced that it is one of the most important aspects of loving my family. I pray God will continue to cultivate this within me, allowing me to reflect his gracious nature to my children.

One of the ways the Lord has allowed me to better understand grace-based parenting is by looking at the Biblical example of the opposite; namely, selfish, works-based parenting.

In Genesis 25, about 20 years after Isaac marries Rebekah, God answers Isaac's prayer and Rebekah becomes pregnant with twins. Even as womb mates, they are struggling with one another, foreshadowing their relationship, and leading us to the Lord's words in verse 23, that the twins will yield two divided nations and the older will serve the younger. We see a partial fulfillment of this struggle at the delivery. The older son, the firstborn, Esau, comes out, covered in red hair, while Jacob, the younger, the second born, follows right after, holding onto Esau's heel.

These two twin brothers could not be more different.

Esau was hairy. Jacob was smooth.

Esau had red hair. Jacob did not.

Esau was a skillful hunter, while Jacob stayed quietly at home.

Esau was favored by his father, but Jacob was favored by his mother.

Why did his father favor Esau? The Scriptures tell us. Isaac loved Esau because Esau earned his love. He earned his father's love by hunting delicious game, affording his father his favorite food. By requiring his children to merit his approval, Isaac welcomed a works-based gospel into his home, ushering in decades of division. Jacob deceives both his brother and father, Esau plots to murder Jacob, and Isaac's own wife shows more regard for her youngest son than her husband; all because the should-be spiritual leader of the home exchanged selfless, grace-based parenting for selfish, works-based parenting.

If you want to divide your home, then allow favoritism. If you want to preach a works-based gospel to your family, then demonstrate love based on what they do for you.

We are desperate for Gospel Families who replace works-based favoritism with the grace-based Gospel of Jesus Christ.

The Gospel of Jesus is a Gospel of grace, and so Gospel Families will be families of grace. I continue to struggle with this concept and am daily growing in my practice of this type of Gospel parenting.

To show grace to my children doesn't mean that I don't have any rules or that I never discipline. It doesn't mean my children are allowed to do whatever they want whenever they want. It simply means:

- That I try to make sure their obedience is not boiled down to a list of "rights" and "wrongs."

- That they have the freedom to live without "walking on egg shells."

- That they know I love them and there is nothing they could ever do that would change that or hinder my love for them in the least.

- That we forgive quickly and freely.

- That I ask for forgiveness too.

- That our prayers are less about behavior and more about the heart.

- That our joy is not dependent upon circumstance.

- That we champion relationship more than rules and discipleship more than politeness.

- That our hopes for them are not based on other people's expectations of them.

- That the grace we show is undeserved and does not, therefore, have to be earned.

- That we show grace because we know grace. Our grace extended is a reflection of the grace received from Jesus Christ our Savior.

My wife has modeled this sort of parenting better than anyone I know. Some time ago, she wrote a blog for our Gospel Family website about parenting with grace, and I want to share it with you now:

Temper Tantrums, Sin & Grace (blog written by my wife, Jessica Williams):

The screams of anger and defiance pierced the joyous reception happening in the church house where my husband pastors. No amount of reasoning, threats of spanking, or bribing calmed the situation. There were looks of awe and horror from those witnessing my 3-year-old child thrashing around in my arms, screaming, and throwing the biggest fit I have ever seen any child throw... and then it happened.

I officially became that parent. I became the parent that can't control her own children.

As I made the quickest exit I could with my unruly daughter I prayed no one would be in the parking lot. I struggled to strap her in the car seat as she struggled to be free from me. I climbed in the front seat and hung my head in shame, in exhaustion, in absolute frustration.

This was the fourth day we had been dealing with this newfound attitude and defiance. The fourth day of trying new ways to "fix" the problem. We tried talks about bad choices, rewards for good behavior, spankings, time outs, taking away beloved toys. We tried it all! I didn't know what to do, or how to parent her. I didn't recognize my own daughter.

Her fit only escalated in the car and I got angry. I yelled. I spoke of the punishment that she would endure when daddy got to the car. She just continued to scream and kick and scream some more, and then, exhausted, I gave up. Defeated, I gave up trying and finally began praying for the situation. I prayed as she continued to scream, and kick, and spew her anger at me. As I finished my silent plea for help, I believe, in that moment, God gave me a glimpse of her through His eyes. In that moment, I saw my daughter struggling. I saw my little girl struggling with sin that so easily entangles and it broke my heart. I was no longer angry at how her fit was affecting me, I was grieved at its affects on her. I was grieved my baby was enslaved to sin and it reminded me of how we all are desperately in need of a savior, whether we are 3 or 33.

I quietly and calmly began telling her how much I love her and how God formed her in my tummy and gave her to our family. I talked to her about the first time I held her in my arms at the hospital and how she is a blessing to our family. As I shared with her, she began to calm down, the anger and frustration seemed to melt away. She stopped screaming, and she just listened. She asked me to tell her more and so I did. We laughed at how she used to call balloons "yappy dooeys" and we discussed how much her brother adores her and how he is her best friend. I told her how special she is to God and this family. We talked about how everything she does not only affects her, but also our entire family. We talked about the sin (bad choices) in our lives that displeases God and hurts those around us.

The tears began to fall from her eyes and through her sweet little sobs she told me she was sorry. She said her brain wants her to do bad things but she wants to do sweet things. I looked into her big blue eyes and told her I understand. I told her that I struggle with sin too and then I told her I forgave her. We talked about how we need

Jesus to help us. I asked her if I could pray for her. She said yes through her tears and bowed her head. I prayed a prayer of thanks to God for loving us even though we don't deserve it. I prayed God would forgive us for our sin and help us make good choices that please Him.

After we prayed her daddy got to the car quite surprised to see a joyful mommy and repentant daughter. He and I discussed her punishment with her and how there are consequences for sin. She remained calm, took her firm punishment well, and then we left the church together telling stories and laughing.

I could have easily missed this precious moment with my daughter to show her grace, to point her to Christ. Like many times before I simply disciplined for an outward change in behavior, not an inward heart change. I was so concerned about how her attitude and disobedience affected me and those around me, that I failed to truly see its affects on her.

As I reflect on the events of this day I believe I need to stop being surprised when my children sin. They are sinners. They need Jesus. They need their mama to seek the Lord in prayer when disciplining them. They need me to speak to them firmly but with grace and in love.

Is it hard? Absolutely!

My flesh wants to discipline much differently than the Spirit within me wants me to.

My flesh is concerned with people's opinions of me as a parent but the Spirit reminds me that, "If I am still trying to please people, I would not be a servant of Christ." (Galatians 1:10)

My flesh is concerned with raising little Pharisees that act good in public but the Spirit reminds me, "The Lord does not look at the things man looks at. Man looks at the outward appearance, but the Lord looks at the heart." (1 Samuel 16:7)

My flesh is concerned with using tactics like yelling and guilt to get my point across but the Spirit reminds me that, "His kindness leads us to repentance." (Romans 2:4)

One thing is certain: I need the grace of God! I need the grace of God to allow me to see my children through his eyes, to discipline in love with a desire to see a heart change, and to show them the life-changing grace of Jesus Christ.

Family Discussion Questions

1. What is the most challenging aspect of parenting?
2. Would you describe your children as blessings from the Lord? Why or why not?
3. What aspects of your child's life or future have you yet to dedicate to the Lord?
4. How can we parent with both discipline and grace?
5. What is your greatest prayer for your children?

PART THREE

Cultivating
Family Worship

CHAPTER 9

For the Glory of God

Pastor Matt Chandler describes *worship* as "The way of life for those entranced by and passionate for the glory of God." Chandler writes, "We worship God when, while we partake of his good gifts, something occurs in the deepest parts of our soul that forbids glory terminating on the gift itself or on our enjoyment of it but that runs deeper into and extends out to the Giver."[30]

The Families of the Nations

Worship music was common in my home as a child. My mom is a worship leader, and would begin "warming up" pretty early on Sunday mornings. I remember waking up to hear her playing the piano and singing songs like "Blessed Assurance," "Because He Lives," and "Shout to the Lord." By the time I got to the church house for our Sunday morning service, I had already sung all of the songs in the bulletin.

Not all expressions of Family Worship will involve Sunday morning hymns on the piano. One of my friends leads his family in worship by teaching them about the Old Testament feasts as they celebrate these meals, such as the Passover Supper. Another man I know plays his guitar while his wife sings praise songs, while one of my Indian friends leads a weekly Bible study in his apartment so that five or six families may read the Scriptures, pray, and sing in three different languages.

I believe that in all of these expressions, when families exalt Christ together, cultivating worship in the home, God is glorified. And as Isaiah 43:7, 1 Corinthians 10:31, and the first Westminster Catechism all agree, "Man's chief end is to glorify God."

The first time Psalm 22:27 captured my heart, it ignited a passion in me to see all peoples turn to the Lord and worship him alone. In fact, that's exactly what the first part of the verse promises: "All the ends of the earth shall remember and turn to the Lord." I longed to see this, and, by God's grace, years later, I was privileged to see the beauty of this promise. I served as a missionary among a people group who had never called Christ their Lord, and was blessed to see them turn to him.

One of the men in this tribe who turned to the Lord was a chief of one of the villages. This man, Danielle, rejected the Gospel the first two times we shared it with him. On our third visit to his village, however, the Amazon *rain* forest lived up to its name as rain poured down, leaving us secluded in our hut. On that wet night, Danielle came to our hut. We talked through the Gospel again and that night, he put his faith in Jesus Christ.

I delight in the promises of Scripture that announce the salvation of people from every tribe and tongue; verses like Revelation 7:9: "After this I looked, and behold, a great multitude that no one could number, from every nation, from all tribes and peoples and languages, standing before the throne and before the Lamb, clothed in white robes, with palm branches in their hands, and crying out with a loud voice, 'Salvation belongs to our God who sits on the throne, and to the Lamb!'"

Families of all tribes will cry out to Jesus Christ in worship for eternity.

Since our church in Houston, Texas is a multi-ethnic church of about 50 nations, I get to see a glimpse of this each week. It's breathtaking to see the nations worshiping together. It's something that many might think impossible. I mean, how could so many cultures, with so many differences—varying languages, an array of music styles, clashing backgrounds, and conflicting traditions—find unity in their worship? I don't believe it's because we're on this side of the Civil Right's Movement but, rather, because we are on this side of the cross. In the midst of all of our differences, we have something in common, something so powerful that the nations can come together united, not by culture, but in Christ.

And this is where the second part of that Psalm 22:27 verse is amplified.

The first part quickens our hearts toward the Great Commission, while the second part awakens the church to the way in which this commission is fulfilled; namely, through the salvation of families.

"All the families of the nations shall worship before you" (Psalm 22:27).

I love the word used here: "families." I know that there will be many families who reject the Gospel, but in a chapter that begins from verse one with a foreshadowing of the cross, how appropriate to find a promise of families worshiping the Lord together in unity.

To cultivate Family Worship is to lead your family to embrace a spirit of unity, unified to the end of glorifying Christ.

Jason Helopoulos writes, "Regardless of who makes up our family, it should be our desire and practice to gather together regularly for worship."[31]

Why is this so important? Why should we invest so much time and energy in cultivating Family Worship? What practical benefits or blessings could our families experience if this were a steady practice in our home?

Helopoulos gives nine practical benefits of Family Worship:[32]

1. Family Worship "centers home."

2. Family Worship "encourages our children in Christ."

3. Family Worship "encourages Christian character."

4. Family Worship "encourages peace in the home."

5. Family Worship "binds the family together."

6. Family Worship "provides common knowledge."

7. Family Worship "equips our children for corporate worship."

8. Family Worship "reinforces spiritual headship."

9. Family Worship "provides systematic discipleship."

The day after that tribal chief, Danielle, gave his life to the Lord, he stood up in front of the rest of the village, in front of his entire family, and proclaimed the Gospel. About a dozen of his family members were saved that day. We baptized them in the river and they began to meet and worship as the church and as a family.

When the Gospel fills the nations, it fills the homes of the families of the nations. And when the Gospel collides with the families of the nations, families all around the world begin to worship Jesus.

Families after God's Own Heart

In the Book of Common Prayer, Psalm 67 is referred to as "A Song of God's Blessing" and recited at evening prayer. It's a short chapter, but I would summarize the Psalm by saying, "God's blessings overflow to the ends of the earth for his glory among the nations."

This is God's heart for the nations. The bottom line, the priority, the driving force, the primary purpose of all God does is his glory. God blesses so that salvation will come to the nations so that the nations, all the earth, will know of his way and praise his name. When the peoples, tribes and tongues come to know him as Savior, they come to glorify him as Lord.

The Psalmist cries out, "Let all the peoples praise you." He shares God's heart for the nations. He longs to see all peoples praising the Lord.

Do we follow this example by sharing God's heart for the nations? Are we a people after God's own heart? Are our homes "homes of worship"? Is our greatest desire to see the nations praising God? Do we demonstrate this passion by worshiping God with all of our hearts? Are our hearts pursuing a genuine time of praise when we gather as a family to worship?

If worship is about us, we are not a family after God's own heart.

If worship is something we can take or leave, we are not a family after God's own heart.

If worship is something we think nations can attribute to whatever god they desire and it's still worship, then we are not a family after God's own heart.

If worship is something we fail to model for others then we are not a family after God's own heart.

If worship is not a natural overflow of all of the blessings we have received from Christ then we are not a family after God's own heart.

If worship occurs only when we are comfortable, happy, and pleased with the events of that week, then we are not a family after God's own heart.

Are we a family after God's own heart?

If worship is focused on an audience of One, then we are a family after God's own heart.

If worship is something we refuse to neglect, something we expect to take place every time we get together, then we are a family after God's own heart.

If worship is our regular response both to the blessings and trials of this life, then we are a family after God's own heart.

Sacrificial Worship

Family Worship is a high calling, for while it is one of the most enjoyable ways a family could ever spend time together, it is also one of the most difficult practices to develop. It can seem strange, sitting around the living room, singing songs to Jesus with just the few people in your home. Families will often find Family Worship to be inconvenient and too demanding on their time. If it were not challenging, a bit uncomfortable at first, then many more Christian families would have already cultivated this corporate spiritual discipline.

The church has discussed spiritual disciplines for centuries, but we typically explore individual spiritual disciplines. We'll consider prayer, fasting, solitude, simplicity, stewardship, and Bible study. Usually, though, we are referring to one believer developing these disciplines in their personal walk with Christ. We need to also champion corporate disciplines, enjoyed by groups of believers, whether the church body or a Christian family. This includes the corporate discipline of Family Worship.

Paul reminds Timothy to "train yourself for godliness; for while bodily training is of some value, godliness is of value in every way, as it holds promise for the present life and also for the life to come" (1 Timothy 4:7-8).

When my wife convinced me to train for a marathon with her, I experienced, firsthand, both the value and challenges that come with bodily training. We would spend our evenings at the Trinity Trails in Fort Worth, Texas, running up and down the winding path flowing alongside the calming Trinity River. Those were some of my favorite, most exhausting dates with my wife. I couldn't go very far at first; perhaps a mile or so. After a few weeks, though, my endurance improved and I could run two or three miles. A few more weeks went by and I found that four miles wasn't impossible, and by the time we ran the marathon, we were logging anywhere from five to seven miles each night and another ten to fifteen on the weekend. Granted, my wife had to carry me on her back for some of those runs, but it was amazing to see just how quickly our bodies adjusted to the distance.

Spiritual disciplines are similar, for they are like spiritual muscles that must be strengthened with consistency and patience. We begin slowly, getting our feet wet in the waters of Family Worship, believing that we will mature in this discipline over time, allowing it to become more and more a part of our family and our daily routine. Family Worship, like physical discipline, will stretch us beyond our normal range into a realm of sacrificial obedience.

Worship will always require sacrifice, for worship is always sacrificial.

We see this truth vividly demonstrated in the familiar story of Abraham and his son, Isaac. In Genesis 22, God calls Abraham to do the most difficult thing imaginable. God commands him to take his son...his only son...whom he loves...and offer him as a burnt offering. This verse always affects me. As a father of two sons, I know I am called to do the same thing. I'm called to give my boys to the Lord. I'm called to trust them in his hands. Just as Abraham was prepared to offer his son as a sacrifice, fully believing that God would then raise him back from the dead (*see Hebrews 11:17-19*), I am to model this faith in God as I dedicate my sons to him as well. I am to follow Abraham's example, for when commanded to offer his only son to the Lord, Scripture tells us that Abraham "rose early in the morning" to obey (Genesis 22:3).

He didn't disobey, and he didn't delay.

They began their journey that early morning and walked for three days. On the third day, Abraham took his son and told the rest of the men there, "Stay here with the donkey; I and the boy will go over there and worship and come again to you" (Genesis 22:5).

There are two amazing things about Abraham's statement here. First of all, he is expecting to offer his son as a sacrifice, and yet he says they will both return down the mountain. This, of course, reveals his faith that the Lord will keep his covenant through Isaac, as promised, and will, therefore, raise up Isaac from the dead after the sacrifice. What faith! What hope! What trust!

The other spectacular truth here speaks powerfully to our topic for this chapter: worship. God told Abraham to offer a sacrifice. Abraham has the knife and wood and is ready to give his offering. But when he heads up the mountain, he tells his servants that he and Isaac are going to "worship." He doesn't say they're going to offer a sacrifice. He says they're going to worship.

Is Abraham confused? Has he forgotten what the Lord commanded him? Is he losing his mind? Is he lying to avoid discussing the painful act of sacrificing his son? Or is it that he knows something about worship that maybe we have yet to learn? Could it be that Abraham understood that worship is more than singing songs and playing music? Could it be that he knew that worship is sacrifice? That worship should always cost us something?

Worship isn't about us. It isn't about our favorite type of music, our favorite praise song, our favorite hymn, or whether or not we are "moved." If it's about us, it isn't worship, for worship is about ascribing worth to the one who is worthy. It is about Jesus Christ, which means we are to sacrifice our own desires, sacrifice our own preferences, and sacrifice our own comfort in order to exalt the name of Jesus. This is why Abraham could talk about worship and sacrifice in the same breath.

When King David went to purchase the threshing floor in order to build an altar for worshiping God, the owner of the land offered the threshing floor for free, at no cost. But David responded, "I will not offer burnt offerings to the Lord my God that cost me nothing" (2 Samuel 24:24).

Family Worship will never be easy. It will always require sacrifice. It will always cost us something. If we mean to gather our family for times of worship, if we aim to lead our household to worship Christ and exalt his name regularly, we will have to sacrifice time, comfort, and schedules. Oh, but let us remember, and let us celebrate, that this sort of discipline is far greater than physical discipline, for this discipline, Family Worship, will prove to be a Kingdom investment with eternal blessings.

5 Ways to Cultivate Family Worship

1. Champion a view of the Sabbath by spending one day a week spiritually resting with your family, forgoing work and busy schedules in order to intentionally make time for praise.

2. Take at least one family retreat a year where you get away from your regular city and schedules by finding a weeklong or weekend getaway filled with slow mornings of sweet prayer, long evenings of worship, and an opportunity to be spiritually refreshed together.

3. Fast from electronics and social media. Choose a day or a week or a month to fast, as a family, from TV, iPads, Facebook, cell phones, and the internet. Let the time that is usually spent online be devoted to Family Worship instead.

4. Write a worship song together. Have your family list attributes of God, favorite Scriptures, and blessings they've received from the Lord. Then have fun finding ways to sing some of these. You might not play an instrument or feel like a gifted singer, but you can still enjoy leading your family to be creative in praising God for what he has personally done in your life.

5. Pastor and author, Voddie Baucham summarizes the simplicity of practically applying Family Worship, writing, "Family worship isn't a full-on church service every day; instead it's a brief time of devotion before the Lord. The elements are singing, Scripture reading, and prayer. You sing together, pray together, and read the Scriptures together. Giving fifteen to twenty minutes a day to these simple practices will transform your family."[33]

Family Discussion Questions

1. In what ways did you see worship in the home when you were growing up in your parents' home?

2. Did you grow up in a home that taught the Bible regularly?

3. Did you grow up in a home that shared meals together regularly?

4. Do you feel confident enough to lead your family in acts of worship (Scripture reading, teaching Scripture, prayer, singing songs of praise)?

5. What fears or concerns do you have about leading your family in worship?

6. What would it look like if your family worshiped together regularly?

7. What blessings do you believe would come from this?

CHAPTER 10

With a Spirit of Joy & Rest

Burnout

MY DAD USED TO SAY, "First you do what you have to do, then you do what you want to do." Others say, "Work hard, play hard." There's some wisdom here circling around work ethic, priorities, and avoiding laziness and procrastination.

In our culture today, however, we rarely get to the "play hard" part of the equation, for there's always more work to do. Our to-do lists are never fully accomplished, our inboxes never empty, and our calendars are always full.

We live with no margin, assigning a name to every second of the day.

People used to come home from work. Now, we come home and work. People used to take vacations. Now we take our projects on vacation. Between our computers, tablets and smart phones, we're always connected, always available, always working.

What ever happened to a Sabbath rest?

Does that sound lazy? Does the idea of taking a break from work seem sluggish? Can we even fathom the thought of being still to delight in the presence of God?

Family Worship must consist of a Sabbath rest: an intentional retreat from the non-stop demand of overtime, kid's sporting events, school meetings, and birthday parties.

The Lord gave his people a Sabbath's day rest. Jesus said, "The Sabbath was made for man, not man for the Sabbath" (Mark 2:27). It's a gift. A gift that we need. A gift that we can't afford to ignore.

We all have busy schedules and full calendars, but unless we push pause in order to enjoy our Savior, rest in the presence of the Lord, and celebrate Family Worship with an undivided, undistracted heart, then I'm afraid that the next thing on our calendar will inevitably be "burnout."

Living with Joy and Margin

If we are to reach for a home of joyful worship and spiritual rest, we are going to quickly realize just how difficult this is in our culture. When it comes to joy, there are a million things waiting to rob us of our joy. My Facebook news feed alone is enough to leave me feeling depressed. In between my friends' status updates and links to YouTube videos about cats, I see seemingly countless articles about all of the tragedies and dangers of our world. Things like kidnappings, terrorist attacks, terminal illness, and human sex trafficking, remind me daily of the heartache of this fallen world. It's enough to land a massive uppercut to your joy before you even leave the house in the morning.

Joyful worship can exist in this wicked, hurtful, broken world, though. Joyful worship is not dependent upon the positive or negative nature of our Facebook news feed. True joy, the kind of joy Paul talks about in Galatians 5, comes from the Holy Spirit within us, not the world around us. This is the sort of joy that Job maintained as he mourned the death of his children; the joy Paul and Silas nurtured as they worshiped from the depths of their prison cell; the joy Jesus pursued while being tortured on the cross (Hebrews 12:2).

The Bible points us to the source of this sort of joy, declaring, "In your presence there is fullness of joy" (Psalm 16:11). We find joy when we find Christ. Family Worship, joyful worship, will take place, then, when we are delighting in the presence of God. If we regularly spend time with Jesus, then we will joyfully walk through storms and suffering, as the Spirit within bears the fruit of joy even among the hopeless weeds of this world. At the same time, we will find joy commonly out of reach whenever we find ourselves commonly out of his presence.

I believe one of the greatest aspects of Family Worship is delighting in the presence of our Savior together. This means resting in him. Now resting in the Lord is as challenging in our culture today as maintaining a joyful spirit. For just as the depressing events of the week crowd our joy, anxious worry impedes any potential spiritual rest.

Americans typically live with no margin. Whatever money we earn, we spend, and often times, we spend more than we earn. Whatever time we have, we spend, frequently filling every hour of the day, every day of the calendar, with something. And to top it all off, in the midst of this margin-less life, we find worry and anxiety filling our hearts. How in the world can a home crippled by anxiety while rushing from one thing to the next, ever enjoy resting in Christ together?

Jesus calls us to rest. He created the world in such a way to model a Sabbath rest, and later tells us that the Sabbath was made for us; for our benefit and blessing (Mark 2:27). Jesus gave us a practical example of restful worship when he visited Martha's home in Luke 10. Martha started so well. She invited and welcomed Jesus into her home. She even spent the day serving him. She resigned herself to the kitchen to wait on the

Lord, while her sister, Mary, plopped down on the floor next to Jesus to listen to his teaching.

Martha's busyness in the kitchen left her with no margin and lots of anxiety. She even became frustrated enough to interrupt the conversation in the living room and demand that Jesus order her sister, Mary, to help her in the kitchen. Instead of complying with her wish, though, Jesus called Martha to exchange her anxiety for the good portion Mary had received simply by sitting at the feet of Jesus. It was the spiritual rest that was blessed, not the spiritual effort.

A Gospel Family will seek this rest as a form of worship, delighting in the presence of the Lord, leaving margin in their schedule for Family Worship. And resting in the presence of Christ, these families will discover the fullness of joy.

Worship Reveals Hearts

One of the sweetest blessings that is brought forth through Family Worship is the privilege of hearing and seeing the hearts of those in your home.

My daughter, Gracie, likes to listen to music when she goes to bed at night. For some inexplicable reason, her song of choice the first three years of her life was Chuck Berry's *Johnny B. Goode*. My mom used to dance with Gracie to *Oldies Music*, and apparently, Gracie had danced to *Johnny B. Goode* with my mom and seemed to think it had something to do with her daddy. So, for three years, this song played on repeat for hours every single night. We have a baby monitor in her room, which meant my wife and I got to hear this song over and over and over again too. I think I could go the rest of my life, never hearing *Johnny B. Goode* again, and be quite content.

I finally reached my breaking point with Chuck Berry and told my daughter we had to get some new songs. I had tried this before and she had always seemed so heartbroken that I ended up caving. Again, I, for the life of me, cannot explain why she was so passionate about this song. Fortunately, my wise wife stepped in and suggested that we make Gracie a new CD filled with some of her favorite worship songs, as well as some new ones. It would be a great opportunity to teach her praise songs, while preserving her father's sanity. Since Gracie had several worship songs she loved—songs like, *Jesus at the Center* and *Whom Shall I Fear*—my wife was able to get her excited about the new CD.

We sat down with my computer one night and made the CD together. My wife and I would play worship songs from our iTunes playlists for our little girl so that she could help us choose which praise songs would make the CD. It was a fun project and everyone was involved. After awhile, Gracie said, "Daddy, put this song on the CD." Then, she just started singing. The problem, though, was that she was singing a song I had never heard. She was singing a song no one had ever heard. She was making it up as she went. It was a worship song. It was about Jesus, but it wasn't in my iTunes playlist.

When she finished singing, I tried to explain that I couldn't put it on the CD. She suggested I just type the words she was singing and that it would then be on my computer. Just before I tried to tell her why that wouldn't work, it occurred to me that I could record her singing and put her track on the CD. So that's just what we did.

I launched QuickTime, hit record, and my baby girl started to sing, making up her own worship song as she went. It's the last track on her worship CD and by far my favorite. It's 38 seconds of my Gracie pouring her sweet heart out to Jesus Christ. There are not many other ways I could have ever heard my four-year-old's heart for Jesus so purely, other than worship.

Gracie has given me permission to share the lyrics of her song:

"Jesus, I need you forever,
You're never gone,
I need you for the whole wide world.

You're more powerful than me,
We need you more than anything,
You're stronger than the computer.

You can do anything,
You're powerful and strongest.
You can do anything,
You're stronger than me."

When families worship together, families receive the rare and precious gift of hearing and seeing one another's hearts for Christ. We still have a monitor in Gracie's room and every now and then this song will wake me up. I'll hear her voice singing and think that she has woken up and is talking. I look at the video monitor to see that she's still asleep and am reminded that it's just the song on the CD. It's just a recording of my baby girl singing to my living Savior with all her heart; a recording I'll always have; a song I'll always remember; a reason I'll keep holding onto as I consider the importance of Family Worship.

Family Discussion Questions

1. What threatens our spiritual rest?

2. What fills our schedules?

3. Is your worship best described as "joyful?" Why or why not?

4. Do you find yourself too busy to focus on Family Worship? What would need to change for you to

have more time to devote to cultivating Family Worship?

5. Who do you know that does this well?

6. What other Bible passages speak to worship?

7. Read Colossians 3:16-17: "Let the word of Christ dwell in you richly, teaching and admonishing one another in all wisdom, singing psalms and hymns and spiritual songs, with thankfulness in your hearts to God. And whatever you do, in word or deed, do everything in the name of the Lord Jesus, giving thanks to God the Father through him."

    a. What are some practical things you could lead your family to do in order to model this passage and practice this type of worship?

CHAPTER 11

In Worship Overflow

An Appropriate Response

WHILE EATING FAJITAS WITH MY wife the other day, I asked her what she thinks of when she thinks of Family Worship. She immediately responded, saying, "Family Worship is giving God the glory he deserves." Jess then gave an example from our daughter Gracie.

A while back, our whole family was sick. It was one of those viruses that you pass around the house, one person at a time. My two-year-old son, Silas, went first and spent about three straight hours throwing up and another 24 hours in bed with mild fever. About the time all of his sheets were washed for the 11th time, my wife took her turn. It hit her a little harder, requiring more hours and leaving a higher fever. The baby and I went last, but before we shared in the fun, Gracie welcomed the virus into her little system.

Fever and nausea engulfed our four-year-old, and I just knew we'd be doing more laundry in no time. Instead of running to the bathroom, however, Gracie lay down, rolling around, feeling sick, and began to pray. She simply asked the Lord to make her feel better and keep her from throwing up. I thought it was cute. She believed it was answered.

Sure enough, about 10 minutes later, Gracie felt fine, her fever subsided, and she never threw up.

While I was sitting there relieved, Gracie turned her heart back to prayer, praising the Lord for healing her and thanking him for answering her prayer.

This is the spirit of Family Worship: it is an overflow of praise to the glory of God; an appropriate response to his faithfulness, provision, goodness, love, and answered prayer.

Family Worship is giving God the glory he deserves while leading the rest of our household to do the same.

It's pointing out God's beautiful sunset while riding bikes to the park. It's praying before a meal, acknowledging that he is our provider. It's singing worship songs and hymns as a family so that our kids are more familiar with "Holy, Holy, Holy," than "Let it Go," the song from the Disney movie *Frozen*. It's helping our families see how Christ is moving in our homes and how he guides us each day.

As the Psalmist wrote, "We will not hide them from their children, but tell to the coming generation the glorious deeds of the Lord, and his might, and the wonders that he has done. He established a testimony in Jacob and appointed a law in Israel, which he commanded our fathers to teach to their children, that the next generation might know them, the children yet unborn, and arise and tell them to their children, so that they should set their hope in God and not forget the works of God, but keep his commandments" (Psalm 78:4-7).

We are called to declare the glorious deeds of the Lord to our children so that the next generation will know and hope in God.

When worship is overflowing out of our hearts, it becomes a part of our everyday life. Giving the Lord glory becomes the norm. We will begin to notice that all of the blessings we have received are gifts from God, allowing us to begin turning those blessings back into worship. It's like filling a glass of water to the brim. Anyone who bumps into it will get a little bit on them. When worship fills our hearts to the brim, it overflows and spills over onto everyone we run into.

New Mercies

One of the ways our families can respond to our glorious God in worship is to simply enjoy the beauty and gift of his character. We can lead our families to take great comfort in the Scriptures that paint spectacular pictures of our awesome God and then respond in overflowing worship.

There's a verse in the Bible that celebrates a truth I have come to treasure: "The steadfast love of the Lord never ceases; his mercies never come to an end; they are new every morning; great is your faithfulness" (Lamentations 3:22-23).

New mercies every morning.

As the sun rises, we rise, with another chance to encounter, all over again, the mercy of our Lord. No matter how we ended yesterday, we begin today with an invitation, welcoming us to delight in the fullness and presence of a merciful, loving, faithful God.

Families are fickle. Our character, volatile. We never know what we're going to get from one another. But God is not this way. He is steady. He is dependable. He is constant. He doesn't choose some mornings to be merciful and faithful and loving. This is his character. This is who he is, and so every morning finds him loving and faithful and merciful.

Every morning, God is who we need the most, giving what we need the most.

Every morning.

Every single day.

We wake up, in desperate need of mercy, and, in the Lord, we find mercy.

We wake up, in desperate need of faithfulness, and, in the Lord, we find that "Great is his faithfulness."

We wake up, in desperate need of love, and, in the Lord, we find steadfast love.

I've yet to meet a family that doesn't share this desperation. I've met families that are unaware of their desperation for all of this, but the more they talk about their lives, their desires, their frustrations, their hopes, and their homes, the more clear it is that their greatest need is the Lord and the gifts he brings with every new morning.

I make mistakes daily. As a husband, as a father, I get it wrong more often than not. Far too frequently, my days would play better as a blooper reel than a highlight reel. The chapter closes, I go to sleep, only to wake up just in time to see that a new chapter has begun. The author of the story is already writing the first lines, and these sentences are filled with words like, "new," "mercy," "never ceases," "steadfast love," and "faithfulness."

I might not always wake up feeling successful in my pursuit of Gospel Family, but I will always wake up to a merciful, glorious God, which means, I will begin every morning with reason to worship; and my family will too.

Jaiden's Story

When I first moved to Houston to pastor Wilcrest Baptist Church, I met a young 7-year-old boy named Jaiden. Jaiden was a special boy with a wonderful family. He had a great smile and a contagious laugh. He also had cancer. I never knew him before his cancer. I never saw him before the treatment had made his face swell. And yet, I never missed getting to hear his heart for Jesus, for no amount of cancer could change that.

Jaiden loved Jesus. He would talk about him every time I visited him in the hospital. He would tell me about his favorite worship songs and all about how he imagined Heaven would be. He even asked me to baptize him so that he could show the entire church that he belonged to Jesus. So I did. With his entire family there celebrating with us, I baptized Jaiden. I'll never forget his baptism.

I remember that the heater for the baptistery was broken and it was a chilly day. The freezing water cut through me as I waded in the baptistery. I almost told Jaiden to wait, though I'm not sure what I would have done to change the temperature. Before I could think, though, Jaiden followed in after me and let out a loud screech as the icy water covered his body. He came close, looked out at the church body, and professed his faith in Jesus Christ.

A few weeks after his baptism, Jaiden was back in the hospital. I went to visit him again and had the chance to pray with him and his mother. Before I did, though, this 7-year-old boy told me something I'll never forget.

Jaiden said, "Pastor Jonathan, when I get to Heaven, Jesus will give me a crown. But I'm going to take my crown and lay it down at his feet, because I love Jesus more than that crown."

I wept.

Right there by his hospital bed, I wept. Right there holding the hand of a 7 year old who understood worship better than I did, who loved Jesus more than anything, I wept. Worship was flowing over, spilling out of his heart, and filling that room. And Jaiden was our worship leader.

Jaiden passed away about a month later, on Christmas Eve, and I imagine that today he and his crown are both at the feet of Jesus.

Family Discussion Questions

1. Who do you know that does a good job of leading others to praise Jesus?

2. Why is it important for families to worship together?

3. What are some ways you could begin to lead your household to worship Jesus Christ together?

4. What worship songs are most familiar to your family?

5. What are some reasons your family has to worship Jesus?

6. What keeps you from worshiping together?

PART FOUR

Cultivating Family Missions

CHAPTER 12

Great Commission Families

Join the Story

EVER NOTICE HOW WE ARE all storytellers? From the old man exaggerating the size of the fish he caught last weekend to the teenager recounting their favorite movie scene-for-scene, we all love to tell stories.

Go through a day and count how many stories people tell you. Look at Facebook and see how many stories and shared stories pop up in your news feed. Stories are all around us.

My kids are definitely storytellers. When I get home from work, they don't just run up and ask me to play with them. They run up and ask me to join a story. They have a role, they assign me a part, and suddenly we're pirates locked in a swordfight or searching for hidden treasure. We're superheroes saving the day, or a royal family attending a ball at the castle.

They've been playing these games for hours before I get home, but once I walk through the door, I'm invited to join the story. Like an actor receiving his cue, I walk on stage and become a part of the show.

Every family has stories that we are a part of everyday.

Most of the time, we sort of stumble into various roles of unintended stories. But what if we were able to choose our family's story? What if we were able to offer our home the role of a lifetime? A big story. A story bigger than ourselves. A story that stretches us beyond our normal roles and reaches further than we could reach on our own.

What if we allowed a God-sized story to captivate our family, inviting us into the script the Lord has written?

What if we submitted our plot, our dialogue, our setting, and our character development to the Author of Life?

I believe that's when our stories would become something we could have never imagined before: stories of hope, transformation, missions, joy, worship, and life.

We have the chance to join the greatest story ever told, still being told, for when Jesus gave us the Great Commission, that was our cue to walk on stage, and join the show.

Make Disciples of All Nations

In the story the Lord has invited our families to join, our role is to make disciples of all nations. This is the Great Commission of Matthew 28, delivering some of Jesus' final words while revealing Jesus' heart for all peoples. Jesus declares his authority over all things, promises to never leave or forsake those who follow him, and commands his followers to spend their lives making disciples. This is a calling that the church still carries today.

While this is a high calling, Jesus bookends this command with his personal assurance. He first says, "All authority in heaven and on earth has been given to me. Go therefore and make disciples of all nations" (Matthew 28:18-19). Before sending his disciples to make disciples, Jesus tells them that he has received all authority. Jesus then uses the word, "therefore," indicating that this command is in light of his authority. We are to make disciples *because* Jesus has full authority, and we are *able* to make disciples because Jesus has full authority. It isn't our authority, our gifts, our talents, and our experience that makes it possible for us to be a part of the Great Commission. It is the power and authority of Christ.

I said Jesus bookends the mission with assurance. Just as he begins with the assurance of his authority, he finishes the call with the assurance of his presence, promising, "I am with you always, to the end of the age" (Matthew 28:20). We go because he is able, and we go because he goes with us.

We've examined our role in making disciples within our homes, teaching our families to love the Lord with all their heart, soul, strength, and mind. Now, we are going to see how these discipled families can live out Jesus' words of Matthew 28 and become Great Commission Families.

Great Commission Families begin by recognizing that Jesus calls us to make disciples and we are able to make disciples through Jesus. After telling his followers to disciple the nations, Jesus promised to send the Holy Spirit to empower them to be his witnesses to the ends of the earth. Most families are overwhelmed by the invitation to be a part of all the Lord is doing around the world. This invitation affords families an expectation, though, that they will not be alone. Not only do we have the assurance of Jesus' authority and presence, we also carry the promise that the Holy Spirit will empower us.

It is natural to feel overwhelmed, stretched, and outside of one's comfort zone when embracing the Great Commission, but, praise the Lord, this mission is not dependent on us and our power. The success of this mission does not rest on our effort or comfort or resources. Our limitations do not limit the Lord's ability to use us and send our families to the broken world around us with his saving message.

Whether or not your family has yet to seek ways to engage this broken world through the power of the Spirit at the command of Christ in order to make disciples of the nations, it is likely that your family has noticed the need for more disciples of Christ in this world. Perhaps, you have even mourned the brokenness of the world around you. You have driven the streets of your city and seen the dark corners. You have talked with your neighbors and discerned hurting hearts. Nightly news programs have reminded you of the depravity of man, while your own sin points to a continued need for the light of the Gospel.

We hear people all the time talking about changing the world. Entire presidential campaigns have been built on the theme of *change*. People respond to this. We respond because, deep down, I believe we all know that this world needs to be changed. It's not difficult to convince people that this is not the way it was meant to be. Something went wrong. Something fell. Something changed and needs now to be changed again. In the same way, we delight in the promise that faith is powerful to move mountains, for, deep down, we all know that there are some mountains that need to be moved.

Blessed to be a Blessing

When God called Abram in Genesis 12, he promised that through his descendants, all nations would be blessed. Paul calls this the *Gospel*, for it brings the good news of one who would come through the lineage of Abram and bless every nation. One would come who would bless the thousands upon thousands of people groups in this world. This descendant would bless the Karamojong of Uganda, the Amarakaeri of Peru, the Dinka of Southern Sudan, the Tamil of India, the Kashubians of Poland, and, as Revelation 7:9 reminds us, "A great multitude from every nation, from all tribes and peoples and languages."

It's clear from Genesis 12 that God made a promise to Abram. We have to look to the New Testament, however to fully understand how God fulfilled this promise; to see how

God blessed all nations through Abram's descendant; to learn the identity of this descendent. Peter and Paul make it clear for us. They make it clear that the descendent is Jesus Christ. He is the one who blesses all nations.

Peter addressed the people, saying, "You are the sons of the prophets and of the covenant that God made with your fathers, saying to Abraham, 'And in your offspring shall all the families of the earth be blessed.' God, having raised up his servant, sent him to you first, to bless you by turning every one of you from your wickedness" (Acts 3:25-26).

God blesses the nations through this covenant by sending His Son, Jesus Christ to turn the nations away from their wickedness.

Paul also emphasizes Jesus' blessing for all peoples, writing, "And the Scripture, foreseeing that God would justify the Gentiles by faith, preached the gospel beforehand to Abraham, saying, 'In you shall all the nations be blessed.' So then, those who are of faith are blessed along with Abraham, the man of faith" (Galatians 3:8-9).

God blesses the nations through this covenant, which is the Gospel, by justifying the Gentiles by faith, so that all who believe in Jesus will be blessed. This is the church. A Gospel Community. A church of the nations, for Christ died for the nations. And the nations continue to be blessed through Jesus as the church fulfills the Great Commission, making disciples of all peoples.

We are a conduit of God's blessings. What he pours into us, we pour into others. We are comforted, so let us comfort the hurting. We have been healed, so let us encourage the brokenhearted. We are forgiven, so let us be the first to forgive. We are loved, so let us love. Let us love our neighbors, our enemies, and the least of these.

One of my favorite things to do with my wife, Jess, is to go skiing. We don't see snow or cold much in Houston, Texas, so we count it a blessing to get to the beautiful mountains of New Mexico or Colorado and spend a week bundled up, skiing through the soft snow.

Since we don't ski often, we don't own our own skis. So, we rent. We go to the clubhouse of the ski resort, wait in line, and then rent boots, skis, and a helmet. We don't rent the skis so that we can just stay there in the clubhouse. It would seem absurd to put on all of our gear just to sit by the fire and drink hot chocolate while we look out the window to watch others ski. We rent the skis so that we can take them all over the mountain, leaving tracks in the snow on every hill.

In the same way, Jesus doesn't save us and bless us just so that we can stay in the church house feeling good about our salvation, drinking hot chocolate by the fire. He blesses us so that we will carry those blessings all over the world leaving tracks of the Gospel on every hill, in every village, in every home to the ends of the earth.

Just like Abraham in Genesis 12, we have been blessed to be a blessing. We have every spiritual blessing as Christians, and that is to overflow in such a way that the nations come to know of the Lord's salvation.

Allow Room for Passion

If we encourage our families to bless the nations the way Jesus has blessed us, then we must allow room for passion. We must allow room for passion because this sort of mission is lived by passionate people. I especially think this is a needed charge for parents, because we are far too often the most likely to quench the passion of our children.

I believe a Great Commission Family will recognize that our children's passion can be a gift rather than a curse. This passion can be a blessing that blesses others.

Kids are wild. They run, they scream, they explore. My daughter sprints everywhere she goes. If she needs water, she runs to the refrigerator as fast as she can. Shoes? She flies up the stairs. Time to go? She darts past her brother to get to the door. She's excited. She's passionate, and I aim to remember that her passion is a blessing.

It's tempting, as a parent, to try and tame my children. I'm not talking about discipline. Of course we discipline. I'm talking about not stifling their passion, excitement, and joy, just because they're passionate about little things, excited in a loud way, and joyful when I'm trying to get them to go to sleep.

Children spend their childhood being told to sit down, slow down, and quiet down. Then, when they're grown, we complain that they don't take a stand, take initiative, or speak up. We ask, "Where's the motivation? Where's the passion? Where's the drive?" The answer is, of course, we told them to suppress it years ago.

New Testament missionaries were driven by a passion for God's glory among the nations and filled with a boldness to live the mission. Passages like Acts 28:31 and Ephesians 6:19 remind us that there is a need for Gospel boldness. Oh, that we would see the passion of our children and, instead of pushing it back, we would cultivate it, encourage it, and lead our children to become passionate and bold for the things of Christ!

I pray that our children would become burdened for the things of the Lord. That a Gospel need in our broken world would capture their hearts and move their feet to respond. That we would not wonder what happened to their drive years from now, for we will, even now, give them room to run, room to love boldly, room to sprint to the hurting, room to fly to the nations, and room to dart to the least of these for the glory of Christ. That we would see the passion of the next generation and view it as a needed gift for which we are desperate.

On January 8, 1956, five American missionaries were martyred for their faith in the Ecuadorian jungles of South

America. One of these men, the one whose name has become the most recognizable over the past 50 years, was a 29-year-old man named Jim Elliot. Just a few years after I gave my life to the Lord, I chanced upon the published journals of Jim Elliot. I was challenged by his spiritual devotions and inspired by his heart for the unreached. When the Lord called me to be a missionary to an unreached tribe in the South American jungles, I turned my attention even more to Elliot's journals and biographies.

In his biography I read about his parents. They were Christians but struggled with the idea of sending their young son to an unknown, dangerous place. It's easy to discuss Family Missions and advocate the idea of being blessed to be a blessing while calling one another to obey the Great Commission inside and outside the home. It's much more difficult when a Great Commission Family is led to go to the unknown or even send their children there alone.

Jim Elliot wrote a letter to his parents, encouraging them in their call to be a Great Commission Family. He wrote:

> "I do not wonder that you were saddened at the word of my going to South America. This is nothing else than what the Lord Jesus warned us of when he told the disciples that they must become so infatuated with the kingdom and following him that all other allegiances must become as though they were not. And he never excluded the family tie. In fact, those loves which we regard as closest, He told us must become as hate in comparison with our desires to uphold His cause. Grieve not, then, if your sons seem to desert you, but rejoice, rather, seeing the will of God done gladly. Remember how the Psalmist described children? He said that they were as an heritage from the Lord, and that every man should be happy who had his quiver full of them. And what is a quiver full of but arrows? And what are arrows

for but to shoot? So, with the strong arms of prayer, draw the bowstring back and let the arrows fly–all of them, straight at the Enemy's hosts."34

Elliot's parents embraced the vision of a Great Commission Family and sent their son like an arrow. Elliot and his wife, along with four other families, gave everything to make disciples of an unreached nation and bless a native tribe with the Gospel of Jesus. That tribe drove spears through the young missionaries before they could ever talk about Jesus. But the Lord's arrow did not return void, for Elliot's wife and other relatives of the martyred men persevered, brought the Good News to the Huaorani, and saw a harvest of souls.

Let our prayer for our family be more than safety. Let us dream beyond the American Dream. Let us join a story bigger than ourselves, and let us passionately resist the temptation to forsake the Great Commission simply because it is difficult or counter-culture or uncomfortable or unfamiliar or unknown. Let us guard our families against the Enemy's schemes as we seek to cultivate Family Missions, for as one author writes, "The Enemy wishes nothing more than to coax our kids, if not into rebellion, into pursuing passionless, insignificant, and potentially empty lives. As long as he can hamstring them with apathy, he need not worry about them doing damage to his kingdom."35

8 Ways to Cultivate Family Missions

1. Buy your children passports. My brother and his wife just did this last year, giving their son and daughter passports for Christmas. While they are leaving next year on a family mission trip, I believe this could be a practical way to move missions to the forefront of your family's conversations, even if you don't have a trip planned.

2. Use your Family Devotion time to walk through the book *Operation World* as a family. This book highlights a different people group every day, sharing national statistics, cultural norms, spiritual needs, and specific prayer requests. If Family Missions includes opening our doors to the nations and the Gospel, we first need to cultivate a heart for the nations and an awareness of the needs of other peoples. Show me a family who prays for the nations and I will show you a family likely to engage the nations with the Gospel.

3. Invite close friends and relatives over for dinner. It is easy to be selfish with our family time. It is easy to guard our nights and weekends to the point that we never share life with others. We come home from work or school, run into the house, lock the door, and pray the phone and doorbell don't ring. When we make time for others and invite extended family, friends, and neighbors over for meals, we often enjoy spiritual conversations and evangelistic opportunities. It is far easier to share the Gospel with those with whom we share life (see 1 Thessalonians 2:8).

4. Invite the lost to your church. In Acts 10, a man named Cornelius put his friends and family in a position to hear about Jesus. For many of us, an easy, practical way to do this is to invite those in our spheres of influence to the church house where they will hear the Word of God proclaimed. There was probably a time before you knew Christ when someone was inviting you to places where they knew you would hear the Gospel. Now it's your turn.

5. Display Bible verses about missions around your

home. We saw earlier that Deuteronomy 6 put forth the model of putting God's Word in our home and the impact this has in our Family Discipleship. What if some of these verses highlighted the Great Commission and God's heart for the nations? We don't put these verses up just for decoration or because they look a certain way or make our families appear a certain way. We can put these verses up around the house, though, to keep God's missional heart at the forefront of our minds, to remind us of the call to be Great Commission Families, and to further cultivate Family Missions in our home.

6. Pray for missionaries. There are missionaries all over the world sharing the Gospel. They, like Peter in Acts 10, walk into homes and story through the life, death, resurrection, and salvation of Jesus. Find a missionary family and begin praying for them. Put their prayer card on your refrigerator. Print out their prayer updates they email and read them to your family during your Family Devotion. Mark their country on the map. Send them care packages and emails of encouragement. Let every member of the family get involved in praying for this missionary family.

7. Sponsor a child through a ministry like Compassion International. Allow your children the chance to get to know this child living on the other side of the world. Let them become pen pals who exchange letters and coloring pages with one another. We sponsor a child in Uganda. We pray for her by name, hang her picture next to pictures of our nieces and nephews, and let the kids help us send her gifts and letters. One of the families in

our church even had the chance to meet the child they sponsor while on a mission trip to Kenya. They spent the day with him, modeling the love of Christ. We hope to take our children to Uganda one day to meet the little girl who has become a part of our prayers and hearts.

8. Go on a family mission trip. Whether it's a local opportunity or an international mission trip, seek a way to engage another culture with the Gospel as a family. My favorite mission trips have been the ones that I shared with my wife, Jess. There aren't many blessings in ministry that compare with the joy of seeing your spouse, firsthand, use his or her spiritual gifts to love the nations.

Family Discussion Questions

1. Who discipled you, taught you the Gospel?

2. How can we disciple others?

3. What is significant about Jesus' mission to not just make disciples, but to make disciples of All Nations?

4. What needs to change in your home, in your heart, for you to become a Great Commission Family?

5. What gets you excited about serving with your family?

6. What passions do you see in your family members that could bless others?

CHAPTER 13

Leading your Family to Christ

A Gospel for All Families

OUR CHURCH RECENTLY SENT A team of 17 on a mission trip to Colombia, South America. I counted it a blessing to be a part of the team, as it allowed me to see Family Missions and Great Commission Families firsthand. We sent three married couples from our church, all of whom spent their time in Barranquilla, Colombia serving together, leaning on the strengths and gifts of one another, making disciples of the nations as a family. Two of our families even brought their children, giving us a total of seven servant-hearted kids on the team. What a joy to see entire families living the mission!

Anytime you enter a new country, you quickly discover unique aspects of the culture from the language and the clothes, to the food and the celebrations. In Colombia, I discovered a new soda drink I had never seen before. It's called *Pony*. Pony is a non-alcoholic malt soda-like beverage sold at the corner stores right next to Coke and Sprite. Children and adults alike seemed to love this soft drink. So, being a good missionary, open to new cultures, I tried it. I bought one, opened the bottle, and took a big drink.

It was horrible. Just awful. One of my least favorite drinks ever. I did not finish it. I did not buy another. But that was not my last time to drink it.

On our final day in Colombia, I was invited into the home of a family down the street from the church we had been partnering with that week. Sitting in the living room with this sweet family, I was getting to know them and trying to share the Gospel through broken Spanish, when I overheard the mother of the household instructing her daughter to go down the street and buy something for me to drink. I immediately spoke up to let her know this is unnecessary, but she merely waved me off, returned her attention to her daughter and told her to go and get me some Pony.

Sure enough, within 15 minutes, I had a full glass of Pony in my hand. Again, I want to be a good missionary and Jesus did say to eat what is put before you (Luke 10:8), so I slowly and painfully sipped my soda. The challenge came, though, when my extremely gracious and hospitable hosts kept refilling my drink with each sip, ensuring that I always had a full glass. Thankfully, one of the women in the room was holding her eight-month-old baby and began to share a cup of Pony with her baby daughter. She loved it. She just kept drinking and drinking that disgusting stuff. Now, as a parent, I was a bit concerned that a little baby was guzzling this soft drink, but then I began to think, the more that baby drinks the less there will be for me to drink.

The baby and I eventually finished all of the Pony in the home and I said my goodbyes. In between sips, however, I, along with one of the women from my church, was able to share the Gospel with this family. They sat on the edge of their seats, asking questions, while clearly welcoming the Lord into their home. They desired a family transformation that only

Christ can bring. It reminded me that, while Pony might not be for everyone, the Gospel is for every family.

There isn't a family in the world that is not desperate for Jesus.

The pastor there in Barranquilla asked our group to lead their church in a three-day Gospel Family workshop. So for three nights in a row we invited the church and the community to come for times of worship as we turned to God's Word and celebrated the call to be a Gospel Family. We walked through Scripture, shared testimonies, and issued a call to cultivate Family Discipleship, Family Worship, and Family Missions. Just as in this book, we spoke of God's blueprint for the family, spiritual leadership, and restoration of a broken home.

The response was overwhelming.

Husbands, wives, mothers, fathers, sons, and daughters, came to us at the close of every night to share their stories and to ask for prayer. Through tears, they expressed their need to have the Gospel in their lives and homes. I heard a man give testimony to his desire to begin leading his family, just before his brother stood up to say the same thing. It reminded me again that this message is for all families of all nations.

One young girl came the first night and said that her sisters and mother were rejecting Christ and refusing to gather with the church. This girl was heartbroken for her family, praying for their salvation.

On the second night, her mom came with her, and her sisters joined them the third night. On that night, I sat with the entire family and just shared the Good News of Jesus and his power to forgive sin and change families. It moved me to see the Lord moving in this family.

Less than 24 hours later, one of the women from my church, Margarita, walked to their home and shared the Gospel again. The entire family believed in Jesus and began following after him.

Many of us are like that young girl. We have members of

our family—spouse, children, relatives—who are lost. The Great Commission can prove challenging for families, but it can stretch us even further when our family members are the lost and broken people we hope to engage with the Good News.

This mission of sharing Christ with families of the nations follows the New Testament example. As Pastor Chua Wee Hian points out, "The apostolic pattern for teaching was in and through family units (Acts 20:20). The first accession of a Gentile grouping to the Christian church was the family of the Roman centurion Cornelius in Caesarea (Acts 10:7, 24). At Philippi, Paul led the families of Lydia and the jailer to faith in Christ and incorporation into his Church (Acts 16:15, 31-34). The 'first fruits' of the great missionary apostle in Achaia were the families of Stephanas (1 Cor. 16:15), Crispus and Gaius (Acts 18:8; Rom. 16:23; 1 Cor. 1:14). So it was clear that the early church discipled both Jewish and Gentile communities in families."[36]

Opening the Door to the Nations

I believe that a family striving to cultivate Family Missions will find opportunities to open their home to the Gospel and engage those closest to us with the Good News of Jesus, recognizing that it is Good News for all peoples.

In Acts chapter 10, we find a man named Cornelius. While he was a God-fearing man, he did not know Jesus Christ. He receives a vision from an angel of God, instructing him to bring Peter to his home. While Cornelius doesn't know what Peter will do or say, he clearly understands that Peter will bring a message from the Lord.

When Peter arrives, Scripture tells us he went into the home of Cornelius and found many persons gathered. You see, Cornelius was expecting a word from God, and had, therefore, called together his relatives and close friends.

Cornelius didn't want to keep this message for himself. He wanted the Gospel message in his home and he wanted all of his family and relatives and close friends to hear it, too. The house was packed with Gentiles, all waiting to hear from God.

Can you imagine following this example? Can you picture your family reaching out to your closest friends and relatives and making a way for them to hear the Gospel? What could you do to open your front door to your sphere of influence? How could your family welcome those closest to you—no matter what background, culture, or nation—into your home and create an opportunity for them to hear about Jesus Christ?

Peter shares the Gospel with Cornelius and his entire family. He preaches that God shows no partiality but saves families of all nations. He walks through Jesus' testimony declaring that Jesus, anointed with the Holy Spirit, performed miracles during His ministry, was crucified on the cross and buried, raised from the dead on the third day, appeared to many witnesses after his resurrection, and gave his disciples the command to make disciples of all nations. Peter then looks at this house filled with Gentiles and boldly cries out, "Whoever believes in Jesus will receive forgiveness of sins." "Whoever!" Not just one group of people. Not just one tribe. Not just one type of family. Not just one demographic of households, but "Whoever!"

After they hear the Gospel, we see Cornelius and his family believe the Gospel, receive the Holy Spirit, proclaim their faith through baptism, and worship God.

This is Family Missions: Bringing the Gospel into the home and then responding to the Gospel by exalting the name of Jesus Christ together.

We need men and women in our homes today to be like Cornelius by opening the doors of their homes to the nations and to the Gospel. And we need more Acts 10 Peters who share this message with the families of the world.

Desperate for our Family's Salvation

In his book on *The Puritan Vision of the Christian Life*, J.I. Packer applauds the Puritan method of spending themselves for the salvation and spiritual growth of their families. He writes, "It was at home in the first instance that the Puritan layman practiced evangelism and ministry."[37] Packer continues to unpack this family ministry, quoting the 17th century Puritan, John Geree, who further described the Puritan's view of Family Missions: "His family he endeavored to make a church, laboring that those that were born in it, might be born again to God."[38]

Paul passionately wrote about his longing to see his family (in a broad sense), the nation of Israel, come to know Jesus. He writes words like, "I have great sorrow and unceasing anguish in my heart. For I could wish that I myself were accursed and cut off from Christ for the sake of my brothers, my kinsmen according to the flesh" (Romans 9:2-3). In a pure and plain prayer, Paul writes, "My heart's desire and prayer to God for them is that they may be saved" (Romans 10:1).

Are we this desperate for the salvation of our family?

Do we see the spiritual depravity of our family members as an urgent call for us to share the Gospel? Do we believe God can use us to lead our family to Christ?

Pastor Hian contends, "The soundest way for a man to come to Christ is in the setting of his own family."[39]

Spurgeon likewise challenges parents in the evangelism of their children: "He who does not labor and pray for the salvation of his own offspring has good reason to doubt whether he knows the grace of God, himself...The objective of parents should be that children should be saved while they are children."[40]

In another sermon, Spurgeon encourages families with a picture of what could take place when we are faithful with this call: "There are some households where all are saved—how happy they should be—where every son and every daughter, father, and mother are all believers—a church in the house, a church of which the whole of the house is comprised. It is such an unspeakable blessing that those who enjoy it ought never to cease to praise God for it day and night."[41]

Whether or not we are intentional to see this sort of household, a home filled with salvation, we are most likely acutely aware of the need. We see lost family members. We see them struggling with sin and addiction. We see their lives plagued by anxiety and depression. Every family gathering, every reunion, serves as a reminder of the brokenness that exists and the hopelessness of ever experiencing healing or restoration or deliverance or salvation. We see the need. Let us then remember that this is a need found in every family and a need that only Jesus Christ can meet.

It always amazes me just how many people are involved in planning a wedding. It's not just the bride and the groom or even their families, but there are friends, decorators, wedding planners, bridesmaids, groomsmen, musicians, flower girls, ring bearers, bakers, and ushers. There are people setting up, singing, reading Scripture, tossing flowers, and taking pictures. When it's time to say the vows, however, when it's time to put the ring on the finger and kiss the bride, only the groom can do it. We never see friends or family members or the baker coming up to say the vows, put the ring on the bride, or kiss the bride. Only the groom can make this covenant with the bride. Only the groom can bring her into a new family with a new name and a new life.

When we look at the lost hearts of our family members, we are looking at a desperate need for salvation that only the Lord can meet, for only Jesus can redeem his Bride. Only the Lord can welcome one into a new family with a new name and a new life. As Peter boldly preached, "There is salvation in no one else, for there is no other name under heaven given among men by which we must be saved" (Acts 4:12).

Only Christ can save our families, but he has called us to be the witnesses that testify of this salvation to our families. For, "How are they to believe in him of whom they have never heard? And how are they to hear without someone preaching?" (Romans 10:14)

About a year ago, a Vietnamese lady came to my office with her family and asked for prayer. She said that her brother had just died and we needed to pray for him. I thought I misunderstood. Either he hadn't died or she hadn't asked for prayer for him, for I couldn't understand why we would pray for a dead man. I sought clarification and she repeated that her brother was dead and we needed to pray. We needed to pray for her dead brother, she confirmed.

I began to think that maybe he was *pronounced* dead and was still in the hospital. I could wrap my mind around that. I could envision us all going to the hospital to stand by his bedside and pray over him. "Is he at the hospital?" I asked. She immediately responded, "No. He's dead. He's at the funeral home."

Now I began to picture us at the funeral home, praying over this man as he's prepared for his memorial service.

And that's exactly what happened. This lady said she wanted us to pray for God to bring him back to life. She said she believed God could do this and we needed to pray in faith. Now, I've never seen someone raised from the dead, but I do believe the Lord can do it. I do believe the Bible is filled with true stories of this very thing taking place, and I know that nothing is impossible with God. So, we went to the funeral home.

When we arrived, her dead brother had already been, to her shock, embalmed. He was in a coffin, the memorial service scheduled. I stood there as the family let all of this sink in. I didn't know what would happen next. I watched my new Vietnamese friend as she began to weep for the first time that day. We still prayed together, but as she saw that the Lord was not going to raise him from the dead, she mourned.

She didn't mourn his death, though. She mourned the fact that she would never have another chance to tell her brother about Jesus. She had been praying that the Lord would give him one more day; that the Lord would revive him for just one more conversation. You see, her brother was lost, and her hope for one more day sprung from her hope for one more chance to witness to her lost brother.

It's not always natural to live with a great urgency for evangelism. Sure we can all agree to its importance in the midst of a discussion on missions. It's easy to feel moved to share Christ with our families after reading the story of my Vietnamese friend. Once this chapter is closed, however, once we move on to another conversation, we will find competing voices and distractions vying for our hearts. We will find ourselves dependent once more on the Spirit of Christ within us to be the one who motivates, inspires, and empowers us to be his witnesses to the ends of the earth, the ends of our street, and the ends of our families.

One of the missionaries our church sent with me on the trip to Colombia that I mentioned earlier was a woman, a member of our church, from Côte d'Ivoire (Ivory Coast), Africa. Her name is Madou. Madou's story reminds us of the power of a family member filled with the Spirit and called to bring the Good News to her home. She grew up in Africa, a Muslim in a Muslim family. Her sister was the first to leave the house and leave Africa when she came to the States for college.

A few years later, Madou and her family learned that her sister had left the Islamic faith to follow Jesus. This news was shocking and unwelcomed.

Madou was sent on a mission trip; a mission trip to the States to convert her sister back to Islam. She came here, moved in with her sister, and began her mission. Madou would invite her to the mosque and leave the Quran open on the coffee table. After a while, Madou began to see that this was not working. So, she decided to try another approach. She decided to go to the Christian church with her sister so that she could learn about their teachings and then show her sister all of their errors and just how misled they are.

It wasn't long, however, before Madou found herself impacted by the message she was trying to disprove and drawn to the Christ she was trying to expel from her home. Madou gave her life to the Lord and embraced a new mission. She no longer tries to lead her sister to Islam, but, instead, she prays the Lord will use her to lead her parents to Christ.

Family Discussion Questions

1. What family members shared the Gospel with you as you were growing up?

2. Who do you believe the Lord is leading you to witness to this week?

3. What are some ways you can put your family in a position to hear the Gospel regularly?

4. Do you feel comfortable leading relatives to a relationship with Jesus? If not, what would better equip you for this task?

5. Which lost family members are you currently lifting up in prayer?

CHAPTER 14

Leading others to Christ

The Heart of a Family Mission Vision

"THE CHRISTIAN LIFE IS A family affair, in which the children enjoy fellowship with their Father and with each other. But we must not for a moment imagine that this exhausts the Christian's responsibilities. We are not to be inward-looking and interested only in ourselves. On the contrary, every Christian should be deeply concerned about others. And it is part of our Christian calling to serve them in whatever ways we can" (Stott).[42]

Perhaps one of the best examples of a missional family is found in the New Testament in the home of Aquila and Priscilla. This Jewish couple met Paul in Corinth (Acts 18) after being kicked out of Rome by the Emperor. Since they and Paul were all tentmakers, they began to work together and soon became partners in the Gospel as well. By the time Paul writes his letter to the Romans, he emphasizes his partnership with this mission-minded family, writing, "Greet Prisca (Priscilla) and Aquila, my fellow workers in Christ

Jesus, who risked their necks for my life, to whom not only I give thanks but all the churches of the Gentiles give thanks as well" (Romans 16:3-4). How refreshing to read of a Christian married couple serving together, joining Paul in his mission to the nations! How inspiring to see a family so passionate about the Great Commission and God's glory that they would risk their lives! What a blessing to read of a family so faithful in serving together that "all the churches of the Gentiles" give thanks for this missional couple!

While in Corinth, Aquila and Priscilla have the chance to disciple another believer. Together, as a family, they teach the Word of God to a man named, Apollos. Luke tells the story of this Family Mission in Acts 18:

> "Now a Jew named Apollos, a native of Alexandria, came to Ephesus. He was an eloquent man, competent in the Scriptures. He had been instructed in the way of the Lord. And being fervent in spirit, he spoke and taught accurately the things concerning Jesus, though he knew only the baptism of John. He began to speak boldly in the synagogue, but when Priscilla and Aquila heard him, they took him aside and explained to him the way of God more accurately. And when he wished to cross to Achaia, the brothers encouraged him and wrote to the disciples to welcome him. When he arrived, he greatly helped those who through grace had believed, for he powerfully refuted the Jews in public, showing by the Scriptures that the Christ was Jesus" (Acts 18:24-28).

As a result of making disciples together as a family, Aquila and Priscilla receive the blessing of being used by God to explain the way of God to a missionary in such a way that he is able to disciple other believers, teaching that Jesus is the Christ. It reminds us of the reproducing discipleship that takes place when we are faithful to obey the Great Commission. This is the reproducing discipleship Paul advocates to Timothy:

"What you have heard from me in the presence of many witnesses entrust to faithful men who will be able to teach others also" (2 Timothy 2:2).

It seems that this New Testament family continued to make disciples in the spirit of Family Missions. In Paul's Romans 16 greeting to Priscilla and Aquila, he refers to the church that meets in their house. By this point in their ministry, they apparently are hosting and perhaps leading a house church.

Whenever I see a family in our church serving together, teaching together, going on mission together, I refer to them as one of our Aquila and Priscilla couples. I was reminded of this partnership time and time again over the past four years as our church commissioned so many married couples for international mission trips; couples like Mac and Grace, Javier and Nancy, Mike and Melissa, Dale and Miranda, Yadu and Shelly, Kelly and Beth, Kurt and Jenn, Guy and Leasa, Hector and Rebecca, Le and Linda, Matt and Emily, Jonathan and Esther, Bob and Becky, Jonathan and Jessica, Ron and Stacy, Darren and Jessica, and Paul and Shelle.

If the Gospel is in your home, it should be carried out of your home to the lost of this world. Your history with Christ is to lead others to a future with him.

Leading others to Christ, reproducing disciples, is at the heart of a Family Mission vision.

Stott writes, "There are still millions of people who are ignorant of (Jesus Christ) and his salvation, in every part of the world. For centuries the church seems to have been half asleep. The challenge is for us to be Christians who are wide awake and active in seeking to win the world for Christ. Seek to discover God's will for your life, and be ready to do it, whatever it is and wherever it may take you"[43]

Light to the Nations

Our church commissioned a missionary team to Haiti in 2013, and I was a part of this group. We spent a week partnering with a local church and the orphanage they had started. Our days found us loving on some wonderful children and learning from a loving pastor. The men and women from my church blew me away as they spent themselves, serving, working, tirelessly sharing their heart from sunrise to sunset.

When the sun began to set, the leaders of the orphanage would often turn on generators in order to ensure enough light for the children to eat dinner before going to bed. Some nights, though, the electricity continued to work, negating the need for generators.

The orphanage was located in the valley of a mountainside where the capital city was located. From the soccer field where our team lost daily to the Haitian kids, you could look up toward the mountain and see the homes of the city and whether or not they had electricity that evening. If they did, then we knew the orphanage would too, though it took a few minutes to reach us.

So every night, around sunset, the pastor would look up to the hill to see if there was light in the city. When he saw light, he put the generators away, knowing that in just a few minutes, he too would have light.

This is Family Missions: Living as the light of the world so that the dark homes around us would be able to look at our families and see the light of Christ and know that in just a short time, they too will have light.

Jesus said, "You are the light of the world. A city set on a hill cannot be hidden. Nor do people light a lamp and put it under a basket, but on a stand, and it gives light to all in the house. In the same way, let your light shine before others, so that they may see your good works and give glory to your Father who is in heaven" (Matthew 5:14-16).

I believe God loves this. I believe God loves seeing families shine their light on the nations so that the nations gather together to celebrate his Gospel. I mentioned earlier the diversity of the church I pastor. I shared about the nations that gather together each week. One thing I always share with them, though, is that we are not merely called to reflect the nations. We are not called to just be multi-ethnic. Secular businesses do that. Schools do that. Starbucks can fill a room with the nations.

We are called to do more than just reflect the nations. We are called to reflect God's heart for the nations.

And this is our hope for families too; namely, that through a Family Mission's heart, our homes will reach out to the nations and see that all peoples have a chance to hear the Gospel.

House of Prayer for All Nations

If we're going to be a light to the nations, we will have to allow the Spirit to refine within us a heart for the nations. We've talked about praying and creating a house of prayer, and we've talked about Family Missions. Now, we see how these two overlap. We see how a mission-minded family will seek a house of prayer, not just for *ourselves* and *our* prayer needs, but a house of prayer for all nations.

A while back, our family left the church house and headed for one of the closest Mexican restaurants. As I devoured the chips, my wife ordered lunch for the kids. Once it arrived, my son was ready to spill more rice than he ate and my daughter was already covering her tortilla in enough butter to make this restaurant start charging for butter the moment we left. Before we could enjoy the fajitas, though, we gave thanks for our food. On this particular day, my daughter, Gracie prayed:

> "Thank you, God, for this day. Thank you for Mommy, Daddy, Sy, Elijah and myself. I pray you heal Silas of his pink eye. Thank you for loving us and dying on the cross for us. Help Clint and Missy, Eva and Bliss and baby Ezra, and Micah too. I pray for Micah too. Help us not sin. And please don't let any Pharaohs come. Don't let any more Pharaohs come ever. Oh, and thank you for this food. Amen."

(Quick side note: Gracie recently watched the movie, *The Prince of Egypt*, and has been terrified, ever since, of the godless, violent Pharaoh in the movie. We're working on this).

Now, Gracie's prayers aren't always as long or thoughtful. Often, they are short, consisting of just a brief, "Thank you for this day and this food." However, this prayer was significant. While it might sound just like another prayer for her family and friends, it is actually a prayer for the nations.

We try to spend time, as a family, praying for our friends who are missionaries in different countries. And we hope to encourage our children to pray for these nations too. So, just before we started spilling queso on our Sunday outfits, Gracie prayed for these Great Commission missionaries.

Clint and Missy are our friends who serve in Poland. Eva, Bliss and Ezra are missionary kids in Asia, and Gracie prayed for her buddy, Micah, because he just recently moved with his parents to live the mission in Poland as well.

In Isaiah 56:7, God clearly shares his will to see his house called "A house of prayer for all nations." I believe the application for today's church is twofold: (1) The nations are to gather together and pray with one another, and (2) the gathered nations are to pray for the nations. In the same way, I believe there's an application for today's families; namely, to create a house of prayer for the nations where our families come together to lift up the needs of the nations and the missionaries serving there.

Creating this type of environment starts with the simple step of opening our eyes and hearts to the nations. We start by simply exposing our family to the nations. We talk about other countries, the needs that exist there, and the missionaries who serve there. We look at maps and we put prayer cards on the refrigerator.

Little by little, we incorporate a Great Commission heart into the DNA of our family, so that one day—when I think we're about to have just another, uneventful, fajita lunch—my daughter will lead us into a spontaneous prayer for missionaries among the nations.

Will you Go?

We have Scripture after Scripture telling us to make disciples of the nations, be light to the world, love the least of these, go so they can hear and believe, and witness to the ends of the earth. We have statistic after statistic telling us that there are thousands upon thousands of unreached people groups, having never heard the Gospel. We have example after example of the brokenness and lostness of this world that is desperate for the salvation of Jesus. We have opportunity after opportunity to be a part of the Lord's Great Mission, joining him in his redemptive plan. And yet, far too often, we have excuse after excuse of why none of this is for our family.

Why not you?

Why not your family?

Instead of considering all of the reasons why you can't go as missionaries to neighbors and nations, why not consider all of the reasons why you *should* go? Instead of assuming you will stay while being willing to go, why not assume you will *go* while being willing to stay?

I was reading through some of my old journals the other night and stumbled upon an entry from 2004. I was living in the jungle at the time, staying in a series of villages located on the same river. We lived with one unreached people group in the midst of a jungle filled with unreached people groups. The following thoughts remind me that families who know Christ must consider how to reach families who don't know Christ.

April 27, 2004: *I hear the sound of a boat approaching along the river. Unzipping my tent, I get up and leave our hut to go examine the racket. Walking close to the edge of the cliff, I use my hand to shield the sun from my eyes as I look down upon the disturbed river. Sure enough, a boat is coming.*

The sound of the motor grows louder as the boat draws nearer. It's headed upstream, so the driver is hugging the bank to gain as much speed as is possible when traveling against the strong current. I have to squint my eyes to see if it is this village they aim for. The boat drifts by our makeshift port and I turn to watch it go.

Rounding the following bend, the boat and its faint purr are hidden by the trees. I can only see the fading trail of the ripples created by the motor spinning beneath the surface. I stand at the cliff a moment more, and I wonder of the people in the boat.

Are they woodworkers who have been cutting and hauling for months only to now return to their families? Are they miners in search of gold? Could they be tourists who, with much hope, paid a fortune just for the chance of spotting a jaguar in the Amazon? Or, perhaps, is it a native family of this tribal jungle who have never before heard of Christ?

Now, today, they're on their way back to a hidden village that is filled with people just like them. A village filled with spiritually lost indigenous who have still yet to hear of the Gospel of grace or the loving forgiveness and salvation of Jesus Christ.

So I wonder, who will go to them? Who will bring these unreached the Good News? When will they be sent? How long? How soon? How many trips up and down this river will these people make in their boat before a Christian reaches them? How many more generations will pass by, never giving worship and glory to God? When will they hear of his fame and honor his name?

The river is calm again. The peace restored. Still my heart is heavy; burdened with prayers for and wonderings of the unsaved, unreached, and unknown.

Then I hear, off in the distance, the sound of yet another motor. I glance downstream as far as I can see. A boat is approaching.

Could your family be the next missionary team sent to the unreached? Could your family be the ones to bring the Gospel to the man driving that boat? Could your family become so passionate about the call to make disciples of the nations, so burdened by God's heart for all peoples, that you will spend the rest of your days on mission for the Lord? Could your family live and breathe the Gospel so that your light penetrates the dark corners of every home on your block and every heart in your family tree? Could the next boat meet you, and through you, meet Jesus?

Family Discussion Questions

1. In what ways has your family served together?

2. What opportunities do you have coming up that your family could take advantage of to serve alongside one another?

3. What blessings do you think would come if you engaged in Family Missions?

4. What spiritual gifts are present in your family that could work well together in missions?

5. What is your prayer for the nations, and how could you lead your household to become a house of prayer for the nations?

6. Where is God calling you to go as a missionary?

PART FIVE

Leaving
a Legacy of Faith

CHAPTER 15

There Arose Another Generation

What about Tomorrow?

WHEN WE FIRST LAUNCHED GOSPEL Family Ministries, I told my wife, "My prayer, is simply that the Lord will use this ministry to lead married couples to pray together and families to disciple one another." By God's grace, I have seen these disciplines joyfully cultivated in families, just as I have seen the Lord teaching my own family how to celebrate these things more and more.

Oh, that you and your family would catch this Gospel Family vision and fully experience the blessing of living as a Great Commandment and Great Commission home! If you do, though, how can we be sure that it will continue? How can we be sure that the next generation will also catch this vision? How can we be sure that your Gospel Family will leave a legacy of faith?

This isn't inevitable, and shouldn't, therefore, be assumed. We see this in the legacy of the Old Testament leader, Joshua:

> "The people served the Lord all the days of Joshua, and all the days of the elders who outlived Joshua, who had seen all the great work that the Lord had done for Israel. And Joshua the son of Nun, the servant of the Lord, died at the age of 110 years. And they buried him within the boundaries of his inheritance in Timnath-heres, in the hill country of Ephraim, north of the mountain of Gaash. And all that generation also were gathered to their fathers. And there arose another generation after them who did not know the Lord or the work that he had done for Israel" (Judges 2:7-10).

God's people served him for as long as Joshua and his elders were alive. As long as the generation who had walked through the parted sea and eaten the manna lived, the Lord was praised. Those who remembered all that God had done for Israel worshiped God for all he had done. Once Joshua and the elders died, however, there arose another generation who, tragically, did not know the Lord.

How is this possible? How could a man like Joshua not pass the baton to the next generation? How could our example of a spiritual leader, the one who led his family to serve God and put away idols not ensure this in the homes of those who would come after him? How could the miracles of the plagues in Egypt, the Passover lamb, the parting of the sea, and the conquest of the Promise Land not be told over and over again to the point that every generation knew intimately the Lord and the work he had done for Israel?

Witmer writes, "We are all just one generation away from unbelief. It is our responsibility to pass the truth along to our children. This is no area in which we should drop the baton."[44]

It's not enough to just lead our family to be a Gospel Family.

This must reproduce. This must carry on. As disciples make disciples that make disciples and churches plant churches that plant churches, Gospel Families cultivate discipleship, worship, and missions in the home in such a way that other homes are impacted and the next generation follows the example. This is a legacy of faith.

In the Amazon, I had the chance to go hunting and fishing with the men of the tribe, two things in which I am inexperienced and just plain terrible. So I would frequently be assigned the easiest, least demanding jobs on these hunting and fishing trips, lest I mess something up. One such trip found me and one of the Amarakaeri men in a small canoe in a still lagoon. He was the fisherman, so he stood in the tip of the boat with his bow and arrow, staring intently into the water, waiting for his shot. I, on the other hand, sat in the back of the boat, slowly and quietly rowing us around the edge of the lake.

Every few minutes Victor would wave me to stop rowing and I would grab a branch hanging over from the bank, causing the canoe to stop. Victor would then fire an arrow into the water, piercing a fish every time. We would retrieve the kill, toss it in the boat with the ever-growing pile, and keep moving.

After a few hours of this, Victor waved me to stop and I assumed he saw another fish. Instead, he slowly put his bow and arrow down, never taking his eyes off the water. Suddenly, he dove into the water and disappeared. I just sat there in disbelief. I looked around to see if anyone else saw what just happened. I looked into the water to try and catch a glimpse of my friend, but all I saw was my own reflection. I waited for about a minute and then Victor exploded out of the water, lifted up a huge turtle with both hands and shouted, "We'll be eating turtle eggs tonight!"

I did not enjoy the eggs, but I'll never forget seeing Victor plunge into that still lagoon to get that turtle. The calm lake burst with a splash, sending ripples all across the surface of the water.

When we lead our families to dive into the Gospel so that we can emerge holding a Gospel Family in both hands, we send ripples that can stretch across multiple generations. When we are sanctified by the truth of the Gospel in such a way that we are set apart from the world, living differently than any house on the block, the impact is felt. Like an echo vibrating for miles, the discipleship, worship and missions cultivated in our homes can resonate for years.

Pastor Matt Chandler summarizes the ripple effect, writing, "The first ripple is our personal reconciliation to God. The second ripple establishes the body of Christ, as we are reconciled to each other. The third ripple is the missional posture of the church as we mobilize to proclaim the fullness of reconciliation in the gospel. In essence, we are reconciled to reconcile."[45]

R.C. Sproul Jr. discusses this idea of legacy in the terms of taking Family Discipleship one step further, to another level: "Love, trust, and obey God and teach your children to do the same. We haven't taught our children to do the same unless or until we have taught them to teach their children. We must with sincerity and zeal teach our children to teach their children to teach their children to teach their children and to keep going until the King's return."[46]

Helopoulos puts it this way: "This must be our true heart's desire: that our children might set their hope in God and that they would teach their own children in turn. And that they would set their hope on God and teach their children and on and on it goes."[47]

Passing the Baton

Just before graduating high school, all of the seniors had to write down one piece of advice, based on all of our vast experience, I assume, that would be passed down to the class to follow. Students quickly began to jot down the sort of wise counsel that only a high school senior can give. We wrote all of the tips and hints we could think of that would guide the next group of seniors. Our class passed on pointers like, "Use all of your college tour days," "Apply for scholarships," "Don't oversleep the morning of the SAT's," and "Avoid the chicken fried steak."

Families who are blessed to live out the Scriptures highlighted in this book will undoubtedly feel passionate about seeing the next class of families blessed in the same ways. If only we could make a list that would go in the back of the Yearbook for upcoming generations.

As we reflect on the previous 14 chapters, as though they were 14 different lines of music from the same song, I want to accent one note for each line. I want to present 14 points of emphasis that the Gospel Family can aim to pass on to the next generation of families in hopes that they too would cultivate Family Discipleship, Family Worship, and Family Missions:

1. Seek ways to grow together spiritually while reenacting the Gospel in the home.

2. Cast a bold, God-sized vision for your family.

3. Establish biblical spiritual leadership in the home while highlighting God's presence, clearing out idols, and serving the Lord.

4. Believe that Christ can restore your home through repentance, forgiveness, and healing.

5. Let love characterize your relationships with God and others.

6. Implement regular times of family devotions.

7. Create a house of prayer and intercede for one another.

8. Parent with a spirit of thanksgiving, dedication, and grace that focuses on the heart and discipleship of the child.

9. Develop a home of worship, delighting in Jesus' glorious presence.

10. Enjoy days of Sabbath rest.

11. Spend time remembering how God has blessed your family and then respond in worship.

12. Join the Great Commission as a family, making disciples of the nations.

13. Find ways to put your lost family members in a position to hear the Gospel.

14. Become a missionary family willing to go.

Two Case Studies of Legacy

As we endorse the passing of the baton to the next generation, encouraging a Gospel Family legacy, it is helpful to look at an example of this. We've seen one negative example in the generation that followed Joshua. A journalist and pastor named A.E. Winship in the year, 1900, published R.A. Dugdale's research of the ancestors of a family called, the Jukes. "Jukes" is not the real name of the family but rather a term that represents all of the descendants of one Dutch man born around 1720.

Dugdale traced the details of more than 1200 ancestors of this man, and concluded that "310 of the 1200 were professional paupers; 50 women lived lives of notorious debauchery; 400 men and women were physically wrecked early by their own wickedness; there were 7 murderers; 60 were habitual thieves; and at least 130 other criminals."[48]

While I believe the Lord can transform any family and can break any cycle of sin, it is eye-opening to see the heartbreaking effects of multiple generations who reject the life-transforming, family-transforming Gospel of Jesus Christ.

On the other hand, the positive legacy left by multiple generations of Gospel Families, serves as a tremendous source of encouragement. Fortunately, Winship provides this example in his book as well, telling the story of another family. The pattern of passing the Gospel Family baton to the next generation who passes it to the next generation, reproducing these values over and over and over again, is exemplified in the life, family, and ancestry of Jonathan Edwards.

Jonathan Edwards, the 18th century pastor, theologian, and missionary from New England, shaped the First Great Awakening and provides a beautiful picture of a legacy of faith. While Edwards left little in the form of financial inheritance, his spiritual heritage proved priceless. Winship's research shows that, "If Jonathan Edwards did not leave a large financial legacy, he did impart to his children an intellectual capacity and vigor, moral character, and devotion to training which have projected themselves through eight generations without losing the strength and force of their great ancestor. Of the three sons and eight daughters of Jonathan Edwards there was not one, nor a husband or wife of one, whose character and ability, whose purpose and achievement were not a credit to this godly man. Of the seventy-five grandchildren, with their husbands and wives, there was but one for whom an apology may be offered, and nearly every one was exceptionally strong in scholarship and moral force."[49]

While the spiritual legacy is the one with which we are primarily concerned, Winship's research also shows the mere power of reproducing family values, whether professional, ethical, spiritual, or educational. Edwards was fortunate to pass down all of the above.

Winship continues his description of Edwards' descendants, reporting, "One held the position of president of Princeton and one of Union College, four were judges, two were members of the Continental Congress, one was a member of the governor's council in Massachusetts, one was a member of the Massachusetts war commission in the Revolutionary war, one was a state senator, one was president of the Connecticut house of representatives, three were officers in the Revolutionary war, one was a member of the famous constitutional convention out of which the United States was born, one was an eminent divine and pastor of the historic North church of New Haven, and one was the first grand master of the Grand Lodge of Masons in Connecticut."[50]

In a stark contrast with the Jukes, Edwards' family inspires our families today to ensure a positive heritage. We see in this study the power of the home. We see both the devastation and beauty that can be reproduced by the upcoming generation, and we are reminded of the importance of leaving a legacy of faith.

As Lois passed on the faith to her daughter, Eunice, who passed it on to her son, Timothy, I pray your family will embrace the Gospel Family call so faithfully that Family Discipleship, Family Worship, and Family Missions will find their way into the homes of every generation to follow.

Family Discussion Questions

1. What are some practical ways we can pass the Gospel Family baton to the next generation?

2. What challenges will we likely face while investing in the younger generation?

3. Who did God use to pass the baton to you?

4. Would you describe the next generation of our nation as a generation of faith? Why or why not?

CHAPTER 16

Marks of a Gospel Family

20 Marks of a Gospel Family

1. You have a "spot" in the house where you and your spouse pray together.

2. Worship songs are more familiar than "Frosty the Snowman" and "Rudolph the Red Nosed Reindeer."

3. The children have passports.

4. Hope of restoration exists even in the midst of the darkest days and biggest fights.

5. Spiritual leadership is clear, consistent, and Biblical.

6. Bibles are near the nightstands, kitchen table, or living room.

7. A church body partners with the family on the journey toward a Gospel Family.

8. Mistakes receive both discipline and grace.

9. Children are held in open hands, surrendered to the Lord.

10. Everyone knows everyone's testimony of how Christ transformed his or her life.

11. Forgiveness is more common than resentment, for there is no record of wrongs.

12. Relationships in the home matter more than superficial Facebook acquaintances, and receive more attention.

13. Confession takes place regularly.

14. There is a family prayer journal.

15. The TV is off during dinner.

16. Names, countries, and prayer requests of missionaries are familiar topics.

17. Neighbors are known and their needs met.

18. People outside the family are frequently invited over to the house.

19. There is a willingness to go wherever the Lord may send and obey whatever calling the Lord may give.

20. They delight in the presence of God, enjoy times of worship, and take comfort in the Scriptures.

How about your family? Are you a Gospel Family? If not yet, why not begin today to be the Gospel Family that God designed you to be, desires you to be, and deserves you to be?

CHAPTER 17

25 Family Devotion Discussion Questions

1. How can we better disciple our children? What are their greatest spiritual needs as children?

2. How has the Lord demonstrated his faithfulness, provision, & goodness lately?

3. How can the local church better equip the family?

4. What Scriptures call us to meet needs? Who is a needy person we know that we can love this week?

5. What fuels your passion for missions? What can we interject into our lives and schedules to fuel this passion?

6. Biblically, are we to keep our children away from things of the world or send them as lights to the world?

7. So far, what has God revealed to you concerning his purpose for moving us to this city?

8. What currently distracts you from time with the Lord? What does the Bible say about devotion?

9. What should you be praying for that you have not been praying about?

10. What godly characteristics do you desire to more fully imitate? Why?

11. What are some Bible verses about serving? How can our family serve together this month?

12. What was Jesus' view of Scripture? Where do we see this? How can we imitate his view?

13. What spiritual disciplines are currently your strongest/weakest?

14. How would you explain God's desire for his own glory? What challenges this in our lives?

15. What is the greatest threat to our marriage? How do we guard against these potential attacks?

16. What passages of Scripture have spoken to you lately?

17. What is clear in Scripture about God's will for our family?

18. How has God blessed our family this month? Why did he do that? What is our response?

19. Finish this sentence: God's _____ is still mysterious to me.

20. What makes God's love so difficult to grasp?

21. What encourages you in your walk with Christ the most right now?

22. What are some fun ways our family can live the mission together?

23. Why did Jesus pray that we would be sanctified by the Word? How does the Word sanctify us?

24. Spend some time encouraging one another & then praying Scripture for each other tonight.

25. What is currently causing you stress, worry, anxiety, struggles? How can we submit these to Christ?

Acknowledgements

A GOSPEL FAMILY REACHES BEYOND the home. I have seen this, as the Lord has extended my family to include more than just my household and relatives. He has blessed me with a family of partners in the Gospel who have passionately invested in this ministry and book. I praise the Lord for this team.

The Gospel Family Ministries' board of directors, along with their families, has faithfully championed this vision. I am, beyond words, grateful for Gregg and Tami McPherson, Brian and Brooke Williams, Jonathan and Esther Schinzler, John and Carolina Montgomery, Vanessa and Noe Ortiz, Kurt and Jenn Freeman, and my wife Jess.

My heart and ministry are always fueled by the prayers, support, and encouragement of my wife. I lean on her wisdom and inspiration daily. Living the mission with her is one of the greatest joys of my life.

My father David brought much needed edits to this book, strengthening every page, as Casey Cease and the publishing team of Lucid Books breathed life into the project.

I offer a special thanks to my beautiful children, Gracie,

Silas, and Elijah, for allowing me to tell their stories, whether they know it or not.

Finally, I recognize the wonderful partnership I have with the Gospel Family of Wilcrest Baptist Church. It is my dear privilege to serve as their pastor. Each day with this Body of Believers fills my heart with joy, deepens my affection for the Bride of Christ, and further stirs my desire for God's glory among the families of the nations.

All of these, and so many others, have sweetly fulfilled the words of Romans 12:10: "Love one another with brotherly affection."

Endnotes

1. J.M. Barrie, *Peter Pan* (CreateSpace Independent Publishing Platform: 2014), p. 7.

2. All Scripture references are taken from *The Holy Bible: English Standard Version* (Crossway, Wheaton, Illinois: 2001).

3. John Stott, *Basic Christianity* (IVP Books, Downers Grove, Illinois: 2008), p. 179.

4. Ibid., p. 180.

5. Gregg Matte, *Finding God's Will: Seek Him, Know Him, Take the Next Step* (Regal from Gospel Light, Ventura, California: 2010), p. 171.

6. Rodney Woo, *The Color of Church: A Biblical and Practical Paradigm for Multiracial Churches* (B&H Books, 2009).

7. Piper, John. "The Marks of a Spiritual Leader." *www.Desiringgod. org/articles/the-marks-of-a-spiritual-leader.* January 1, 1995.

8. Timothy Witmer, *The Shepherd Leader at Home: Knowing, Leading, Protecting, and Providing for your Family* (Crossway, Wheaton, Illinois: 2012), p. 91.

9. *Today in the World*, Moody Bible Institute, August, 1991, p. 23.

10. Voddie Baucham Jr., *Family Shepherds: Calling and Equipping Men to Lead their Homes* (Crossway, Wheaton, Illinois: 2011), p. 36.

11. Eric Mason, *Manhood Restored: How the Gospel Makes Men Whole* (B&H Publishing Group, Nashville, Tennessee: 2013), p. 134.

12. Malcolm B. Yarnell III: "My Son, Be Strong in the Grace that is in Christ Jesus: The Baptist Family at Worship." Southwestern Journal of Theology, Volume 49, Number 1: Fall 2006, p. 52.

13. Piper, John. "The Marks of a Spiritual Leader." *www.Desiringgod. org/articles/the-marks-of-a-spiritual-leader.* January 1, 1995.

14. Sally Clarkson, *The Mission of Motherhood: Touching your Child's Heart for Eternity* (Waterbrook Press, Colorado Springs, Colorado: 2003), p. 87.

15. Dr. James Dobson, *Bringing Up Boys: Practical advice and encouragement for those shaping the next generation of men* (Tyndale House Publishers, Wheaton, Illinois: 2001), p. 137.

16. J.I. Packer, *Knowing God* (InterVarsity Press, Downers Grove, Illinois: 1993), p. 122.

17. Ibid., p. 214.

18. D.A. Carson, *The Difficult Doctrine of the Love of God* (Crossway Books, Wheaton, Illinois: 2000), p. 48.

19. C.H. Spurgeon, *His Great Love: Volume 52, Sermon #2968* as quoted in Stephen McCaskell's, *Through the Eyes of C.H. Spurgeon: Quotes from a Reformed Baptist Preacher* (Lucid Books, Brenham, TX: 2012), p. 68.

20. C.H. Spurgeon, *John Ploughman's Pictures* as quoted in Stephen McCaskell's, *Through the Eyes of C.H. Spurgeon: Quotes from a Reformed Baptist Preacher* (Lucid Books, Brenham, TX: 2012), p. 66.

21. Richard J. Foster, *Celebration of Discipline: The Path to Spiritual Growth* (HarperSanFrancisco: 1998), p. 38-39.

22. Richard J. Foster, *Celebration of Discipline: The Path to Spiritual Growth* (HarperSanFrancisco: 1998), p. 39.

23. Anselm, *Proslogion: With the Replies of Gaunilo and Anselm* (Hackett Publishing Company, Inc.: 2001).

24. E. Stanley Jones, *A Song of Ascents* (Abingdon Press: 1968).

25. Richard J. Foster, *Celebration of Discipline: The Path to Spiritual Growth* (HarperSanFrancisco: 1998), p. 39-40.

26. A.W. Tozer, *The Pursuit of God* (Wing Spread Publishers, Camp Hill, Pennsylvania: 2006), p. 28.

27. Eric Mason, *Manhood Restored: How the Gospel Makes Men Whole* (B&H Publishing Group, Nashville, Tennessee: 2013), p. 143.

28. Timothy Keller, *The Reason for God: Belief in an Age of Skepticism* (Dutton, Penguin Group: 2008), p.177.

29. Ibid., p. 178.

30. Matt Chandler with Jared Wilson, *The Explicit Gospel* (Crossway, Wheaton, Illinois: 2012), p. 42.

31. Jason Helopoulos, *A Neglected Grace: Family Worship in the Christian Home* (Christian Focus Publications: 2013), p. 26.

32. This list comes from the section headings of chapter 3, *"How about some other Practical Reasons?"* in Jason Helopoulos, *A Neglected Grace: Family Worship in the Christian Home* (Christian Focus Publications: 2013), p. 41-49.

33. Voddie Baucham Jr., *Family Shepherds: Calling and Equipping Men to Lead their Homes* (Crossway, Wheaton, Illinois: 2011), p. 79.

34. Elisabeth Elliot, *Shadow of the Almighty: The Life and Testament of Jim Elliot* (HarperCollins Publishers, New York, NY: 1989), p. 132.

35. Julie Ferwerda, *One Million Arrows: Raising your Children to Change the World* (Wine Press Publishing: 2009), p. 21-22.

36. Chua Wee Hian, "Evangelization of Whole Families," published in *Perspectives: On the World Christian Movement, Third Edition*; Edited by Ralph D. Winter and Steven C. Hawthorne (William Carey Library, Pasadena, California: 1999), p. 616.

37. J.I. Packer, *A Quest for Godliness: The Puritan Vision of the Christian Life* (Crossway, Wheaton, Illinois: 1990), p. 26.

38. Ibid., p. 270.

39. Chua Wee Hian, "Evangelization of Whole Families," published in *Perspectives: On the World Christian Movement, Third Edition*; Edited by Ralph D. Winter and Steven C. Hawthorne (William Carey Library, Pasadena, California: 1999), p. 614.

40. C.H. Spurgeon, *The Sparrow and the Swallow: Volume 53, Sermon #3041* as quoted in Stephen McCaskell's, *Through the Eyes of C.H. Spurgeon: Quotes from a Reformed Baptist Preacher* (Lucid Books, Brenham, TX: 2012), p. 69.

41. Ibid.

42. John Stott, *Basic Christianity* (IVP Books, Downers Grove, Illinois: 2008), p. 183-184.

43. Ibid., 184.

44. Timothy Witmer, *The Shepherd Leader at Home* (Crossway: 2012), p. 110.

45. Matt Chandler with Jared Wilson, *The Explicit Gospel* (Crossway, Wheaton, Illinois: 2012), p. 175.

46. R.C. Sproul Jr., *When you Rise Up: A Covenantal Approach to Homeschooling* (P&R Publishing: 2004), p. 25-26.

47. Jason Helopoulos, *A Neglected Grace: Family Worship in the Christian Home* (Christian Focus Publications: 2013), p. 36.

48. A.E. Winship, *Jukes-Edwards: A Study in Education and Heredity* (R.L. Myers and Co., Harrisburg, PA: 1900).

49. Ibid.

50. Ibid.

CPSIA information can be obtained
at www.ICGtesting.com
Printed in the USA
FSOW01n0730170815
9835FS